T0208640

A Teacher's Storybook

Expanded Edition—80 Short Stories
With a Special Children's Story at Book's End

Raymond J. Golarz
With Marion Simpson Golarz

authorHOUSE®

AuthorHouse™
1663 Liberty Drive
Bloomington, IN 47403
www.authorhouse.com
Phone: 833-262-8899

Published by AuthorHouse 06/17/2022

ISBN: 978-1-6655-5796-2 (sc)
ISBN: 978-1-6655-5814-3 (e)

DEDICATION

To Our Children and Grandchildren

CONTENTS

Section Two: Ralph, the Tiniest Leaf

Section Three: About the Authors

Acknowledgements

To my teachers:

My father "Lefty" Golarz who taught me the love of storytelling,

My friend Gary Phillips who taught me in the telling,

My wife Marion who taught me how to move from the spoken story to the written one.

PREFACE

My father, the son of immigrants, was a great storyteller. He spent his childhood living through the Great Depression. Thus, he could tell us stories of collecting coal along the railroad tracks to heat one's house, the experiences of being a picker on large farms, and the CCC camps, and the often coming together of a community to help a neighboring family in need. In addition, he abhorred discrimination and racism and had a plethora of stories to tell us of all of these experiences that tore at our hearts and souls.

My first storytelling professional experience took place in Chicago. I was with Dr. Gary Phillips, a respected colleague, as he was presenting an address to several hundred teacher union leaders—not an easy audience. Halfway through his presentation, he found that his voice was so hoarse that he could not continue. He turned to me and said, "Ray, take over." Then he grabbed a chair and sat.

I was terrified. Then instinctively, I began to tell a story—a story about my grandfather, "The Saw Sharpener." It is one of the stories included in this book. It is the story of an immigrant who had no formal education, yet was filled with an understanding of the harmony of God's universe. I followed that story with another—the story of the parent of a handicapped child who once abused her child before she knew about his handicap and his lack of a normal ability to control his behavior. Afterwards, she vowed that neither she, nor anyone else, would ever abuse that child. It's also in this book, "The Advocate."

When I finished my presentation, the audience responded very positively. Soon I was presenting throughout Chicago. Dumas

Elementary School was one of those Chicago schools and the story, "Dr. Golarz, Do You Enjoy Chopin?" came from my experience working there. It is the touching story of a very sensitive, young, black girl who wrapped her warmth around my heart. This story is also included in the book. After Chicago, my career in storytelling really took off. Over a twenty-year-period, I was invited to keynote conferences in virtually every state in America and in every Canadian province. The stories always had a moral theme and, over the years the stories grew in numbers to over one-hundred.

A downside of the keynoting was not being able to tell conference participants where they could find these stories in written form. There were so many times when I had to disappoint participants and advise them that I had never written the stories. Finally in 2017, Marion began to help me in the writing. In 2019 we published *A Teacher's Storybook*. That publication contains thirty of the stories that made up keynote addresses. The only criticism we received from those who read this book was their disappointment of not finding a favorite story included in that publication. We heard comments like "I couldn't find the story about Mike and the starfish. Didn't you include the story about a student who was helped to study the stars?" Thus, the decision to publish A *Teacher's Storybook* as an expanded edition. As I stated, the number of stories had grown to over one hundred. This expanded edition contains eighty of the most popular.

For years, I have grappled with explaining how these stories all fit together. Is there an underlying focused message? Until this year I have been unsuccessful. Then my wife Marion reintroduced me to a prayer that we are all familiar with, and, as if by divine intervention, the veil was lifted. The connection was clear. Virtually all of my stories align beautifully with the message of the words of "The Serenity Prayer."

"God grant me the Serenity to accept the things I cannot change,
The Courage to change the things I can,
and the Wisdom to know the difference."
–Authorship -uncertain

Now, for the stories in this book. We have stated that they each share a moral message. But we understand that one might ask how they are different, yet fit together comfortably with the message of this prayer? Hopefully the following examples will clarify our thinking.

Some of the stories are immensely sad and disheartening because they describe dark human conditions that could not be corrected such as in the stories "Shades of Grey," or "Gaagii." As the prayer suggests, these stories illustrate *the things that require our Serenity because we must accept that which we cannot change.*

You will also find stories expressing courage and God's grace that resulted in a moral victory such as "The Beauty and Power of Compassion," or "Mike the Bus driver," or "Marble Street." These are the stories that speak of *The Courage to change the things we can.*

Finally completing the connection to the last line of the prayer are stories that simply leave you with an unanswered moral dilemma awaiting a resolution such as "Profound Complexity" or "Who Can Judge." As the prayer proclaims, these stories call upon our *Wisdom to know the difference.*

We hope this prayer provides additional insights as you ponder the meaning of each story.

Given the serious nature of so many of the stories, we felt the need to include some stories that are also humorous. I always included some of them when I keynoted a conference. Seated auditorium audiences need that, as I am sure you do too. So, you will find sprinkled throughout the pages any number of stories that have been included not only for their moral value, but also because they are funny. You will run into, "Jebronowski's Horse," and "Hazel," and "The Water Runs Through It." Hope you find them as funny to read as we found them to write.

Almost all of the stories in this book are quite short—no more than a page or two. For those of you who have read some of our earlier books or have read some of our newspaper articles, you may find some of those stories that are also included in this new book. You may or may not recognize them, for all of the stories in this book have either been modified to fit this short story version, or contain elements new to the story. Most of the stories, however, have never been in print.

Section two of the book is a very special caboose. In years past, we have had some parents tell us that some of the stories in our books have been a joy for their children to hear. Parents have, we are told, sat together to read these stories. Therefore, included at the end of this book is a special children's story, *Ralph, the Tiniest leaf.* If you have no child to read it with, reach back into your own childhood and enjoy this very simple read.

In the movie *Spartacus,* Kirk Douglas who plays Spartacus asks Antoninus, a slave who wants to join their rebellion, what or how he can contribute to their war effort. There is initially some concern as to the value of Antoninus' contribution when he answers that he is a "Singer of Songs," in other words a storyteller. Antoninus, sensing that the other slaves and Spartacus are apprehensive about his ability to contribute aggressively, he then declares that he came to fight.

It is not until later over an early evening campfire when he performs his song that tells a story, that all present, including Spartacus, recognize his gift as a unique and necessary contribution to any army. Spartacus then declares to Antoninus in front of all present, "I was wrong about you poet, you will teach us songs. Anyone can learn to fight."

Hope you enjoy all of the "Songs" in this storybook.
RJG

SECTION ONE

THE STORIES

"God grant me the Serenity to Accept
the Things I cannot change,
the Courage to change the things I can,
and the Wisdom to know the difference."

Authorship-uncertain

Some teachers are artists who can masterfully open the treasure box of profound learning. Such was Mr. Nelson. He taught poetry and literature. The poem he selected that first week of class was "Thanatopsis."

THE TREASURE BOX

I recall vividly how he enthusiastically passed out printed sheets of the poem while he danced between the aisles of our classroom chairs—simultaneously sharing in his mellow baritone voice stanza after stanza of Bryant's magnificent poetic gift. With each reading he seemed to go deeper into the poem. It was as if the poem and he were now in a conversation. It was clear that he had created magic. He took us far that day. He had opened a treasure box and invited us to glimpse inside. We had, however, no idea of the depth of the trip he was planning for us.

A week later he took us further. Using the poem, he had us carefully ponder, discuss, and analyze. He guided us into an open conversation of mortality. Finally, cognitively exhausted, we understood Bryant. Or so we thought. But he wasn't finished. He looked at us and said, "My young friends, I have but one final question." We eagerly waited, confident and cognitively ready. Then he said rather unceremoniously, "What would you do if your mother died?" It seemed a strange question and momentarily he caught us off guard, but we regrouped, hands going up. Responses came from all corners of the room: "I'd call other members of my family. They would need to know." "I'd search for insurance papers—we'd need those." "I would quickly write the essential obituary."

While we gave our answers, Mr. Nelson had been moving slowly to the right-front seat in our classroom, a seat occupied by Tony. Tony seldom said much. We all knew he was kind of slow, but no one ever laughed at him. He was perceived as just a big, not-very-bright, nice kid. We had finished our responses when Mr. Nelson arrived at Tony's chair. I remember that he looked directly into Tony's face and in a quiet, gentle voice, he asked, "Tony, what would you do?"

Tony quietly responded, "I'd cry." Mr. Nelson looked up at all of us as the room fell silent. The lid of the Treasure Box had been opened wide by a "not-too-bright" kid named Tony and an artist named Mr. Nelson who, in the silence of that classroom, watched as we all now peered in. He then said, "Bryant meant not for you to intellectually ponder death. Rather, he meant for you to feel. The journey into the poem was not meant to be a cognitive journey—rather a journey to be felt—a conversation not of minds, but of hearts. Now you may leave class early. Walk the grounds and ponder what you may have learned today."

We left class richer that day. Somehow, in that brief moment in that classroom an artist named Mr. Nelson showed us where to find our real humanity, and he did it through the magic of poetry and by pointing out for us the incredible beauty and wisdom existing within, what we had thought, was one of the simpler of our fellow men.

Several of us walked Tony home from school that day where we got to meet his mom and dad. We began to include him in some of our activities. He seemed to like that.

I don't really remember what else Mr. Nelson taught us that year. I suppose those were the "essential" things on the standardized tests.

As an educator you soon learn that if you keep your eyes and heart open you will find magnificence all around you. Thus you will be consistently rewarded with unanticipated gifts.

"Do You Enjoy Chopin?"

It was a very cold, windy, late November Saturday morning with traces of snow in the air as I was completing my drive to Dumas Elementary School on Chicago's South Side. The neighborhood had the look of post WWII Germany with only very old houses, most abandoned—many in disrepair. The few business establishments had iron grates on all of their windows and doors. The occasional oil-drum fires where heavily clothed old men gathered in an attempt to keep warm were the only signs of human occupancy.

I continued to drive. Slowly more houses and businesses came into view. Finally, I came upon a one story brick school building. I pulled up and turned off my car. Almost immediately four fairly good sized men approached and surrounded my car. I was anxious. The largest leaned over close to my driver side window and asked, "Are you Dr. Golarz?" I nodded. In an authoritative tone he said, "Come with us. We're your body guards." In the building, Sylvia Peters, the principal, wrapped her arms around me and said, "Thanks for coming. Welcome to Dumas."

Some months earlier I had agreed to keynote her school's Celebration of Learning. Sylvia introduced me to four of her sixth-grade students—three girls and a boy. She told me, "These children have won the honor of showing you around their school. They all led the entire school and community in the annual candle-light ceremony this year. Please go with them." I nodded and then the smallest of the three girls took my hand, looked up, smiled, and said,

"Dr. Golarz, do you enjoy Chopin?" I was completely taken aback and then responded, "Why, yes, I do." As we walked, the young man chimed in, "Chopin is our composer of the month. All of our language arts and our creative writings focus on him and his music as our central theme. Last month it was Schubert and next month it will be Handel."

As we talked, we passed by classroom after classroom. Each classroom door was decorated with a collage of pictures and historical information which related to a particular composer. I had not expected to experience what I was being shown. Is this the kind of school that our nation defines as dysfunctional? Then Sylvia explained that though the great composers curricular design had brought immense pride to her school and community, it was but one of the strategies designed to facilitate student capacity and their more extensive depth of knowing.

She explained further that she had cajoled local businesses into donating violins, cellos, woodwinds, brass, and percussion instruments so that Dumas Elementary could have an orchestra—a meaningful connection to the composers her students were studying and a touch of class to match the new found dignity of her students and their community. Sixty years of educational research affirms that individual schools are the most effective units of improvement— never state legislatures. Dumas was an excellent example of this.

As I drove away, the neighborhood seemed a little brighter. Most of Sylvia's students were still struggling to read at grade level, most were still hungry when they woke up each morning, and most would never experience a home with both a father and a mother—many with neither parent. But they had a neighborhood public school that offered hope and provided pride.

As for me, I got a special gift that snowy, November morning, for whenever I hear the music of Chopin, I picture the beautiful, proud face of a young African-American girl who captured my heart and said to me with a smile, "Dr. Golarz, do you enjoy Chopin?"

Teaching with its profound impact doesn't happen every day. But when it does…..ah, when it does, how special and often lifelong that impact is. All teachers can tell you about such times, for they are the cherished, lifelong memories of teachers. Following is one such story.

DANNY AND CHARLIE

D anny came to my seventh grade class from foster care, placed
in the school district with a loving family. He could neither
read nor write. He was a tall, gangly, timid boy. I did not know of his
deficiencies until he handed in his first in-class writing assignment.
What he handed in was a page filled with lines of scribbling, blank
space, more scribbling, blank space, more scribbling, blank space,
on and on, line after line. There were no words. My heart ached. It
ached more as I observed him at recess preferring to play with first
and second graders. His foster parents, the principal, and I met.
We did not conclude with a viable plan to help Danny—merely a
commitment to find one.

Several days later on a rainy fall morning when the "walkers"
were permitted early entry into the school building, I observed
Danny sitting on a stair with a classmate, Charlie. Charlie was short
and overweight, extremely shy and very bright. Yet as shy as Charlie
was and as timid as Danny was, they appeared to be enjoying their
conversation and moment of camaraderie. I had been praying for an
opportunity and here it was, so I took it and ran.

After school that same day, knowing that they were both "walkers,"
I asked them to assist me in taking equipment to the park (football
practice field) three blocks away. They talked all the way to the park,
completely ignoring my presence.

A second writing assignment came. I advised Danny that he did
not need to do it. He looked up at me and said, "Coach, if I can find a

way to do it, will you take it?" I said, "Sure, Danny, sure." The day the assignment was due, Charlie and Danny came to me. Charlie turned in his assignment and then the two of them handed me another paper. Charlie explained, "For a week Danny has been making up this story and memorizing it. Yesterday I wrote it for him. He knows he can't write yet, but, it is his story. Will you take it?" I kept that paper for many years. The story was very elegant in its simplicity.

I knew Charlie wanted to do something athletic. So I would occasionally give the two of them a basketball and let them go out on the playground's far end for twenty minutes or so to practice. Eventually, they came to me after school to get the basketball and play until dark.

A treasured memory I still have is looking out of my third floor classroom window and watching the two of them, arm over arm, walking home, a vision that always brings a smile to my face.

Charlie got pretty good at basketball. He was hard to beat at the game of horse. Danny, mostly with Charlie's help, learned to write. Their friendship was lifelong.

There really is no possible way to adequately pay building principals and teachers for the work that they do. For you see, all of what they do may never be known, that is, of course, unless you come to know about it accidently.

THE PARENT CENTER

I t was a spectacular spring day. Over the previous two weeks we
had gotten more than our fair share of mid-America rain, so
the grass that had been waiting all winter was growing, touched
everywhere by spring flowers. As I looked out of my office door that
morning, I could see Johnny, the Director of Buildings and Grounds,
walking briskly through the sun-filled hallway.

"Johnny, found that portable classroom yet?"

I was having a little fun with him. We had twelve portable one-
room classrooms that we moved around to different locations in
the school district as enrollments shifted and we found a need for
additional space. Last year we had been using ten of the portables.
Two were sitting idle. Well, one was sitting idle. The whereabouts of
the second was unknown.

In the school business you get used to having some things
occasionally disappear: library books, a computer, cables needed for
electronic equipment, a basketball, baseball equipment, even once a
fairly sizable, portable soccer backstop—but a portable classroom?
Never lost a portable classroom.

I knew it was a sensitive spot for Johnny, so I let up, laughed and
said, "Johnny, don't worry. We'll find it. I mean, really. How far can
you get with a hot portable? Where would you fence it?" I laughed
again. Johnny just looked up and shook his head.

A week or so later, Johnny and I were visiting some of our
elementary schools in the central city. We were trying to get into as

many classrooms as we could. Teachers never get enough visitors. When they do, they never tire of having their pupils show off regarding something that they had just learned. As superintendent, I always found it to be an uplifting experience. We left the last school on our list of morning visits, got into our car, and as we drove around the school grounds, we marveled at the manicured lawn and beautiful flower beds. The flowers surrounding the new parent center behind the school were particularly well-tended. The new parent center— what an attractive, wonderful welcome gift to the poor parents of this community.

We stopped on the street for a moment of admiration. As we sat there, not looking at one another, Johnny asked, "Ray, what would you estimate the size of that freshly painted, one-room parent center, surrounded by beautiful flowers to be?"

"You mean is it possible that the parent center with the flower boxes under the windows and new white gutters and down spouts is about the same size as a missing classroom portable?"

We parked the car and went into the building to find Nancy, the principal. On the way to her office we ran into her. "Oh, I'm so glad you're here. Have you time to stop at the parent center?"

"Nancy, that's what we need to talk to you about? Can we go to your office?"

"Sure, or we can talk at the parent center. It's not as full now as it is in the morning. Can't even find elbow room in there in the mornings."

"Full? What are you talking about, Nancy?"

"Well, we opened the center about six weeks ago. Within a week, by 6:30 a.m. it was full of young mothers. They found out that a number of our teachers were coming in early to teach a few mothers how to read. Well, they all wanted to learn to read. Run three morning classes now, an hour each, starting at 5 a.m., about twenty in a class. Teachers rotate the teaching of the classes."

"They come at 5 a.m.?"

"Some would come earlier if we were open. If they stay at home, their drunken exes or boyfriends coming in from the bars look to have their way with them, raping them if they don't consent. It's a bad situation in this neighborhood for these young women and their kids. Bad, Ray—really bad. Poor is not a good thing to be in America. But, I'm so sorry. Here I am running off at the mouth, and you wanted to talk to me about something."

I looked at Johnny, then turned to her and said, "It can wait, Nancy. It can wait."

We had our visit at the new parent center, even enjoyed doughnuts made by a few of the teachers. As we passed by the center in our car, we stopped for a final look.

"What do you think, Johnny?" Johnny quietly responded, "Think the portable we're lookin' for is smaller. Matter of fact, I'm sure it's smaller." I looked at Johnny, smiled, nodded my head slowly and responded, "Think you're right, Johnny. Think you're right."

With my master's degree in hand from Indiana University I got a job. I had already taught middle and high school for several years, so I was a perfect fit for the school district's new, federally-funded delinquency prevention effort. They wanted staff that had some teaching experience. I thought I was prepared. I was soon to understand how much I yet had to learn.

The Real World

My first day on the job at 7:45 a.m., I met my mentor at a house in a heavily industrialized part of town. The house was one of the few remaining in an area of condemned houses being razed as a part of a redevelopment effort. I pulled up, and Andy Hiduke was already there waiting for me.

"Have a hard time finding it, kid?"

"No, not really. Just didn't realize there were still houses in this area."

"Won't be for long, kid. Won't be for long."

I followed him up the broken concrete sidewalk to the house. Andy was an old salt—reminded me of some Navy petty officers I had served under, the kind of guys you could work with for thirty years and still not tap all that they knew or could teach you. He had been doing police and court work for years during which time he had been Chief Probation Officer for the Lake County Juvenile Court. He was a crusty, tough veteran who clearly knew his way around the darker parts of the community.

As we cautiously continued down the dangerously cracked and broken sidewalk to the house, Andy turned to me and said, "These are poor but proud people, Ray. This mother will, in her way, have cleaned the house for our coming, but it smells so bad in there that you won't notice her efforts. She may also have gotten a little coffee from somewhere and made some for us. If she offers, accept. She has little else. Their last name is White. They have 14 children. Nine still live in the house. The two eldest sons are doing time at the state penitentiary for armed robbery. The whereabouts of two older girls and another, older son, all dropouts, are unknown."

As we approached the front door, it was opened to us by a barefoot and scantily dressed boy who appeared to be about four years old.

"Hello, Mr. Andy."

Andy replied, "Joshua."

Then we heard from within the house, "Mr. Andy, you just come in here and bring your friend too."

We walked through the living room and into the kitchen. There we found Mrs. White. She was an extremely large woman. I knew from earlier conversations with Andy that she was in her mid-forties, but she appeared to be much older. Life had been hard. "Would you want some coffee?" We accepted and sat. One of the several young girls near the kitchen served us. Andy then advised Mrs. White that I would be working with her and her family. At this she seemed quite distressed.

She turned to me and asked, "Will you remember to bring us a food order if we need one?"

I smile and replied, "Yes, ma'am. I'll remember. I promise."

She returned my smile and seemed to relax. As Andy took over the conversation, out of the corner of my eye I watched a large roach working its way along the kitchen door frame toward a fairly sizable hole in the ceiling. While I continued to glance around from where I sat between the kitchen and living room, I could see in the living room stacks and stacks of disorganized clothing, blankets, bedding, badly-torn furniture, and mattresses. In and amongst these stacks and piles were small half-naked children playing everywhere.

I turned back to the table at the very moment that a large roach dropped from the hole in the ceiling. It landed no more than an inch from Andy's hand that was gripping his coffee mug. He did not move. He didn't in any way act startled. He did nothing to shame or humiliate this poor woman who, though she had little, was attempting to give us her best. He was the most gracious of guests.

As we left the White's house that day and went to our cars, I looked up and said a quiet "thank you." I had come to this job with my new university degree, but I had been taught more on my first day, in an old run-down house, by a seasoned mentor than I ever could have imagined. Andy looked back as he entered his car and with just a trace of a smile on his face, he slowly nodded, then with a knowing look said, "Welcome to the real world, kid. Welcome to the real world."

As I traveled our country keynoting conferences, I found often that I came away with more than I gave. Once, in North Carolina, I was given the gift of this following story.

MIKE THE BUS DRIVER

His name was Mike. He was a school bus driver. His assignment was bussing children in grades one through four. He liked his work—he liked kids. Earlier in life he had been a fighter pilot. A war injury ended his service, but Mike had no regrets. Driving a bus and daily seeing young faces was a good life.

One day a senior administrator asked him to deliver a note to the building librarian. Mike accidently entered an auditorium where a faculty meeting was in progress. Leaving would have created a disruption so he sat down quietly. He intended to leave as soon as he could. While waiting, he heard the principal express a deep concern. "My colleagues, many of our students seem not to appreciate their good work. I know you are aware of this, for you have told me so. I have no immediate answer, so I ask you to assist me in any way you can with some resolution."

The meeting ended and Mike quietly left. Though simply a bus driver, he thought possibly he might help. He had noted for quite some time how his students often left their graded school work on the bus. It had saddened him particularly to see so many of the papers with stars and smiley faces strewn across the floor of the bus. He knew, of course, why they left them, for he knew his route. Most of his students went home to empty houses so there was no one to show these papers to.

Mike decided to do what he thought could be his part. He announced to all of the students riding his bus that he wanted to see their good work—especially the work with the stars and smiley faces. When they did this, he expressed appropriate compliments to them for such work. Then he would sign "Mike" in the upper- right-hand corner of their paper with what he called his "Magic Christmas red pen." Soon Mike found that at the end of his evening run, the bus was much less littered. There were never again papers on the floor bearing stars and or smiley faces. Teachers began to notice that children were requesting more of these rewards and showing an increased willingness to work for them. It didn't take teachers long to find the source of enthusiasm. It did take a little longer for Mike to load his late afternoon bus run, but everyone seemed willing to work around that.

Eventually Mike passed away. The number of young children and parents who came to his funeral was moving. Shortly after his death, an unexpected practice began to occur. Graffiti began to show up on the outside of the bus Mike drove, always a star or smiley face and always in red. Authorities never looked for the perpetrators, nor were the drawings ever washed or wiped off. Eventually, over time, they simply faded away.

My story-teller then told me her name and advised me that she was now a teacher at that same school. Without saying anything else, she very carefully pulled from her purse an old, yet neatly folded paper—her own personal work product from so many years ago. On the paper were a star, a smiley face, and the name "Mike" written in the upper right-hand corner—a name written I'm sure with a "Magic Christmas red pen." She looked up at me and smiled. I nodded my head and smiled back.

It isn't just teachers who make magnificent differences or touch the hearts of us all.

There are so many times that we speak and don't understand the significance of what we say. We don't understand how important, how meaningful or how necessary the words were. Maybe we really can't. So possibly we need to speak and then quietly, ever so quietly, simply be there and then hope that our presence might, for a moment, relieve the pain

CAREGIVERS IN NEED OF CARE

I had been invited to keynote a conference in Phoenix. The day before my address, a fellow superintendent invited me to visit some elementary schools. As we walked through one of the school hallways, we noticed farther down the hall a young teacher on one knee with two second grade boys. We could see that she was attempting to resolve a fight. Tears streamed down the face of one boy. The other still had his fists clenched and a scowl on his face. As we neared, she looked up and said, "I'm so sorry, I'll get them back into class soon." I responded, "You need not apologize. We'll get out of your way."

The next morning I gave my address. Afterwards, several participants approached forming a line. At the back of the line was the teacher who had been working the day before in the hallway with the young boys. When she finally reached me, she said, "Dr. Golarz, may I please talk to you?"

We found a quiet spot outside near a fountain and some very lovely orange trees. She began, "Today in your presentation you said that besides caring for our students, we must also remember to take care of ourselves, the caregivers. I knew when you said this, that I needed to talk to you. Yesterday in the hallway at my school, I knew I should have been in my classroom teaching, but they were fighting and I had to …I had to…" She began to get choked up and was momentarily unable to continue.

I said to her, "Don't ever apologize for the work that you do. Your

21

job always includes assisting children to understand civility. You were doing the right thing." Then she blurted out, "But Dr. Golarz, it happens all the time—all the time! I have thirty-five students in my classroom, seven of whom I cannot control. I've had lots of administrative help, and I've tried all of the new instructional strategies."

She went on to say, "Several veteran teachers have confided in me that no one has ever been able to handle this group. They've told me to just try to make it through the school year. But I don't know if I can. Last Tuesday, I was physically attacked and struck. An older teacher heard the noise and rushed to my aid. It's only October, just October. I can't sleep. I'm losing weight, and I'm jittery all the time. On Friday, the principal and I had a conference with a parent who yelled and screamed at me the whole time. She told me I was picking on her son, that there were other children just as bad, and that I was racist.

"Dr. Golarz, I'm from Iowa. It was my idea to go into teaching. My dad only agreed to my teaching if I kept my other major in business. Therefore, I graduated with a double major and a 3.7 GPA. At night if I call my parents, I can hear my dad hollering in the background. He says that if things don't change soon, he's coming out on a plane, gonna punch some people out and take me home. Dr. Golarz, I so wanted to teach. It has been my dream since childhood."

She took a deep breath, dropped her head, then turned and slowly walked away. She didn't go far, just nearer the fountain in the center of the courtyard garden. I didn't follow. She needed a moment alone.

The orange trees in the courtyard didn't look quite so lovely any more.

Unless we understand the depth of the pain of those who are our fellow men and women, we will assuredly never understand them.

THE ADVOCATE

I had just finished participating in a case conference, the purpose of which was to rewrite an IEP (individualized educational plan) for a special needs fourth-grader in our school system. After the conference I asked Martha, the boy's mother, to join me in my office. Besides representing her son, Martha advocated for many district children. She had an in-depth understanding of special education law and a profound sensitivity for special needs children.

Resources available for special needs children have always been inadequate. From its beginning in the early 1970s the special education mandate has never been adequately funded. Martha, besides advocating for individual children, always helped me with the legislative and funding issues. She was tireless in this regard.

We met that afternoon and plotted some legislative strategies for the coming general assembly session. As we completed our work, I asked Martha if she would mind a personal question. She nodded and said, "Go ahead, Ray." So I said, "Martha, you are a truly extraordinary advocate and you have the persistence of a junkyard dog. Can you help me understand the source of your endless zeal?" She looked at me for a long moment and then asked, "Ray, do you mind if I close the door?" I said, "No, of course not."

She then began, "If a child's special needs are not clearly identified most of us tend to assume he is normal and treat the child accordingly. My son Timmy seemed normal. So, when Timmy transgressed we assumed that he was being defiant or stubborn. By the time he was six, dealing with him alone took ten times the effort and strength I needed to deal with our other children. Jack left for work early each morning and typically didn't get home until 6:00 p.m. By evening each day I was exhausted. If I hadn't slept the night before, I was a zombie. On one of those days I had reached my limit. I grabbed Timmy by his shoulders and then screamed at him. I said, 'Get out, leave this house, go away and don't come back."

When I regained my composure I began to prepare supper. The house seemed unusually quiet. Then something told me to look for Timmy. So I did. I looked everywhere but could not find him. Panic set in, and I went outside searching the neighborhood, now screaming out his name. When Jack got home, I gave him a brief explanation then took his car.

The cold rain was turning to sleet. The car was sliding as I braked on freezing streets. I was driving bigger and bigger circles away from our home. I finally got to the main boulevard. Traffic was heavy. Standing on the corner was this sad and pathetic six-year-old holding a stick on his shoulder with cans of food at the end of the stick wrapped in a bathroom towel. I jumped from the car leaving it in the street and screamed "Timmy." He looked up at me and said through his tears, "I am so sorry, Mommy. I did what you said and left but I don't know where to go."

I grabbed him and hugged and held him. As I knelt there, sobbing and holding him, I vowed that I would never again hurt him—nor would I ever let anyone else hurt him.

A month later, we got his psychological evaluation that included a listing of the behaviors over which he most likely had little control. She said no more.

She didn't have to. We sat silently looking out the window at the setting sun.

Veteran teachers have learned to be prepared for just about anything. Tragically, there are some things that defy preparation.

A Teacher's Worst Nightmare

My phone rang. It was a teacher colleague from California. "Ray?"

"Yeah, Dan."

"You watchin' CNN?"

"No, out having lunch."

"Watch CNN. Our school's on lock-down. I can see two, no, three helicopters. At the entrance way of the building there are police in helmets separating hundreds of black and Hispanic students—fights all over campus. God, hope they can get this under control. DAMN. Shot just fired through a window of my classroom.

EVERYBODY ON THE FLOOR NOW, NOW! Ray, can't talk."

Terror enveloped my soul for Dan, followed immediately by a rush of memories that took me back in time.

The phone was ringing and my secretary Phyllis was screaming to me.

"It's Chief Wise—Police Department."

"George?"

"Ray, we have a full-blown situation erupting on the streets surrounding Central High. We're alerting your school staff, but this thing looks like it will overrun our resources. We'll be calling upon the East Chicago and Chicago police for help. You might want to delay dismissal in some of your surrounding schools until we get this under control."

I hung up, crossed the office area and went directly into the superintendent's office. "John, just talked to Chief Wise. Here's the situation." I explained and then we divided the emergency assignments. Soon we had informed all personnel who needed to know, put into place emergency procedures, and had updated news services. At that point Central High School called and advised us that some of those involved in the rioting had entered the north end of their building. Young adults carrying arms were seen.

With a fellow administrator who had done extensive work with the rioting communities, I drove to the scene. We could see men standing on corners holding hand guns and carrying rifles and shotguns. Many we did not know. They appeared to be older. They were drinking heavily and throwing bottles at passing cars.

We got out of my car near the football field. It was at that moment that I was most terrified, for coming out of a neighborhood of mostly southern whites were seven or eight men. They were carrying weapons of all kinds including shot guns and hand guns. They were moving toward the high school. My terror was knowing that if they walked far enough without changing direction, the corner of the high school building that was obstructing their view would no longer block their sight-line and they would be able to see the armed group of black American men on Calumet Avenue.

At that moment two police squad cars, sirens and lights on, came careening at breakneck speed around the corner from Sohl Street moving directly toward them. The gang of whites fired several of their weapons in the direction of the squad cars and then scattered quickly into the neighborhood. For the next four hours the police, slowly yet steadily, regained control of the neighborhoods and streets.

Somewhere near 7:30 p.m., faculty and staff were beginning to gather in the high school cafeteria. Many were in shock. Some had vomited. Others would soon do so. Others were sitting and shaking, while still others just stared blindly into space. Some teachers who had assumed leadership were moving from teacher to teacher, trying to calm frayed nerves or just hold those who could not stop shaking. They would continue tending to their comrades until all were safely out of the building. The next day there would be no school, nor the day afterwards, nor the week after that. It takes time to bandage psychological bleeding.

My thoughts returned to my friend Dan, and then I said a prayer for teachers everywhere.

I am of an age where I find it entertaining to read through the ever-increasing number of ideas suggesting how to create great schools. Some, like paying teachers more than simply a living wage, or reducing class sizes have merit. Seldom, however, do we get to ideas that are transformative, but we should try.

JOE WENT TO ALASKA

B ill, the president of the teachers association, came to my office. "Ray, I have a request." He then continued. "You know Joe Nelson—biology teacher at Central high school?" "Vaguely," I said. "Well, Joe and I go way back, actually started teaching together some 38 years ago. He was some crackerjack teacher in those days—fire in the belly. Couldn't get him to stop talking about biology, even over a beer. Things change though. Eventually, if, like Joe, you teach long enough, most people don't even remember your name or what you teach. So you tire."

He paused and then went on, "In Joe's early years he had a dream. He wanted to go to Alaska and take pictures and then produce slides of the flora and fauna for his classes. Well, several of Joe's close friends are going to Alaska on a hunting trip this coming September, and they have asked Joe to come along with his cameras. But Joe's personal leave-time is all used up. He used those days when his wife was hospitalized. Ray, would you meet with Joe and several of us from the association to see if we can help him?" I agreed.

Later, the association leadership, Joe, and I met after school in my office. Joe explained his situation. We deliberated. Our deliberation was resolving nothing. The peaceful meeting was becoming tense. Joe politely got up and headed for the door. He turned and said, "I'm sorry, I didn't mean to cause such a problem." I then said something I had not planned. I can only assume that I was guided in my statement by a power greater than me. "Joe, wait. I have four unused personal business days. Take mine." We were all stunned, including me. I turned to Bill. "Will the contract let me do this, Bill?" Bill slowly replied. "I'm not sure. Let us look into it."

They left shortly thereafter. Several days later Bill called. "Ray, we won't need your days, but we do need your assistance. The association leadership has decided to add a new provision to our contract permitting teachers to exchange unused personal leave days. Will you take this to the school board so that they can sign off on it?" "Be happy to, Bill."

Joe went to Alaska with his friends. He did so with five personal leave days given to him by his fellow teachers. He took his pictures of the flora and fauna and created his set of slides. After his return, our school board president asked him to present a portion of his slides at a school board meeting. His presentation was fascinating. He ended with these words. "It's been very long since my work has been so honored. Thank you."

Some say that Joe's last two years of teaching were his best. He taught with a "fire in the belly" that captivated his students and brought rookie teachers to him for guidance. His career ended not with a whimper but with an explosion of excitement. His career ended with honor—as all careers should.

The tragedy of this story is that it is the story that could be told of thousands and thousands of hard working Americans.

Stan and Mary

Stan and Mary were married in 1953. In 1954 Stan went to Korea. In 1956 he came home from the Korean War and got a job working on the Lake Erie docks in Cleveland. It was hard work, but he was delighted to have the job. In 1957 Mary had their first child. Shortly thereafter, she was pregnant with their second. A house become available in a modest neighborhood they liked, and with the financial help of family they bought it.

The house had been constructed in 1938. It was well-built and had a basement, kitchen, dining room, a small den, one bathroom, and four bedrooms upstairs. It needed work, but it would be a home where they could raise their family.

For the first five years after purchasing the house, they bought only the essentials. With any money left over they paid back the relatives who had assisted them with the purchase of the house and also put aside money in the "strike fund." God forbid that the dockworkers would go on strike, but if they did, they would need to be ready.

Eventually, they had six children and they all attended the school down the street, Roosevelt Elementary. It was a working-class school, a school where parents and teachers worked together. Children understood that violating standards would not be tolerated—not at school, nor at home.

Over the years, Stan slowly improved their house. A second bathroom was built in 1960 with the help of Mary's brother and a friend who was a plumber. In 1963 Stan began remodeling the kitchen, giving Mary a double sink, a window that looked out over her back yard, cabinets, and a larger area for the kitchen table. He pretty much finished the kitchen in 1965. In addition, he rewired the basement, built bookshelves in the den, painted and replaced most of the front porch, and put up a two-car garage. With friends and relatives, he laid a concrete driveway on the side of the house that went all the way to the detached garage near the back of the lot. By the time Stan retired, there wasn't much that hadn't been built, rebuilt, repaired, or touched up.

After a long, good life together raising their family in that comfortable home, Mary passed away. Stan, shortly thereafter, kept getting confused, fell badly a couple of times, and then went several miles away to live with a daughter and her husband.

Stan and Mary hadn't saved a lot. They had spent their money frugally while raising a family. Stan had done most of the home improvements by himself or with family and friends. Mary had cooked, cleaned, and helped maintain the condition of their home while she tutored, nursed, and gave individualized attention to a growing and maturing family.

After Mary passed, Stan's only real asset was the house, and now the time had come to sell it. But he felt okay about that. He had kept it in good shape, and its reasonable sale would give to each of his six children a small inheritance while they raised their own children. So Stan and some of his children arranged a meeting at the house with a local real estate agent. The agent began by explain the housing market and what they could expect from the sale of the home.

"Sir, I know the house is in great shape and immaculate but the school down the street has just been given a grade of "F" by the state. So, finding a young family with children or any family willing to buy here will be immensely difficult. You may need to consider asking substantially less and come down at least $40,000, or maybe more, if you want to sell."

Stan said nothing. He just dropped his head, walked slowly to the sink, and looked out of the window that Mary loved so much.

It was now time to say goodbye to the old house and have his daughter drive him back to her home. They stopped for a red light, and from the rear seat of the car he looked out. He could see after-school children laughing and horse-playing as they left Betty J's corner store, chewing their penny candy on their way home, full of hope and joy as his kids and their friends had done so often years ago.

The traffic light changed and they moved on, except for the image of the happy children of his neighborhood that he held in his mind. Stan slowly turned from the window and looked forward. He smiled. Nothing of real importance had really changed in his neighborhood.

Maybe someday someone would explain to him exactly what an "F" school was and why it meant that he now practically had to give his house away.

I taught middle and high school. Many of my students were poor, neglected, or abused. So when an opportunity became available to direct an inner-city poverty intervention project, I accepted. Soon, as when I taught, I was learning more about poverty, abuse, neglect and delinquency than I cared to know. The intensity of my work peaked one snowy, cold, late Friday afternoon in mid- December.

ENDLESS SHADES OF GRAY

I was checking on a referral from the court system. The referral took me to an apartment in an old mansion built in 1880 that we called "the maze." The mansion had been cut up into no-less-than twenty small apartments. Rickety staircases lined the outside of the house, and from a distance the entire structure had the look of braided hair. I found 22B. The door was ajar.

I knocked. It opened into a gray, dark, empty room. Near the back wall was a child about four months old. He was just lying there. His breathing seemed labored. He was wet, shivering and wearing nothing more than a very soiled diaper. I yelled but no one responded. I knocked on other apartment doors. No response. I wrapped the child in my coat and left a note, "Have your baby. Come to the Police Department."

All the way to the Police Department I couldn't get the picture of the apartment out of my mind—no toys, furniture, pictures, nor light—just endless shades of gray. I thought of my own children's bedroom—so different.

I put my hand on the child lying next to me, a child trying to breathe between deep coughs. At the station, Sgt. Wleklinski met me. He took one look at the baby and then asked, "Do you know any Chicago Police that can get us into South Chicago Hospital's pediatric emergency center?" I responded, "Yes." "Then do it."

All the way over to the Skyway through the rapid flashing red and blue lights of the squad car, all I could envision as I held the child were those shades of apartment gray. Poverty creates some indelible images.

The next morning about 7:00 a.m. Wleklinski called me at home. With a trembling voice, he told me that the hospital had just called and despite their best efforts, the little guy didn't make it. He was dehydrated too long. There was too much pneumonia, too much fever, just too much of everything. I thanked him for calling and hung up. I walked to the open doorway of my own children's bedroom. They were all still asleep.

As I stood there watching them with my head leaning against the door frame, a tear ran down my cheek and then several more. I didn't want to cry, but it wasn't going to be something I would decide. There are times when it happens that way. Inside of you, it just hurts.

Later I went back to classroom teaching. I never again experienced such a loss, but I and my fellow teachers were always aware of the many other children in need, like the little girl held affectionately by her kindergarten teacher because she knew that the child lived nightly with physical and sexual abuse, or the kid whose high school teacher always saved him half of her lunch because she knew it would be his only supper, or the really poor kids we all slipped a little money to so for once they could have the dignity of buying their mom a Christmas gift.

So this Christmas season I pray, "God bless, protect, and cherish those who teach and give them needed peace."

As for the little guy, I'm sure God found for him a place of perpetual and everlasting light.

For many years, I worked daily in the impoverished communities of Northwest Indiana and South Chicago. I got to know the culture and the community idiosyncrasies house-by-house, alleyway-by-alleyway, and neighborhood-by-neighborhood. I became familiar with the odors, the loss of hope, the depression, the tears, and the brutality that overshadowed the occasional joys.

CYNTHIA

Prior to my long work with these communities, I thought naively that some people were simply poor. The longer I worked, the more I came to understand that there were no less than two kinds of poor—the poor and the very poor. My daily immersion in their lives gave me a deeper understanding of the endless burdens of those who made up the very poor.

I found as I worked that their lives were desperate not simply because they had no money and few resources, but because they were trapped. Life without viable supports or options had crushed and permanently changed them.

Cynthia was one of the many people I got to know who were among the desperately poor. I first met her when I responded to a neighborhood alert advising that someone might be living in an old, abandoned clapboard garage.

It was mid-January when I cautiously worked my way over ice and snow covered walkways to the backyard structure. The garage door was slightly ajar. I knocked. I knocked again. The door opened slightly. Through this slightly opened doorway I could see a frail and small woman wrapped in a torn blanket. Only her lower legs were exposed and there appeared to be snakes wrapped around and moving on those exposed lower legs. She looked so very sad, cold, and pathetic.

Behind her in the back corner of the garage I could see a cot covered with old rags. There was movement under the rags. As my eyes became more accustomed to the darkness, I could see that the movement was being caused by small children. They were making no noise, simply huddling together attempting to stay warm. Within the garage there were only two sources of light, a single light bulb hanging down from an electrical cord and an opening at the bottom of the back wall where insufficient rags were allowing daylight along with snow to enter the room. I saw then that the snakes on her legs were actually large varicose veins. It is strange how such sights never leave you. Though this occurred many years ago, these images remain burned in my psyche. I later came to know that she had seven children. She was but 23 that cold January day.

As I began to work with Cynthia and her children, I came to know them. One of the first things Cynthia confided to me was that one of her earliest, most terrifying memories was of being repeatedly raped at the age of seven. She thought that these assaults had actually occurred much earlier, but she wasn't sure. She told me that she learned through those experiences never to fight back or resist, for to do so would only result in more beatings. Vulnerable and helpless, she had learned to become quiet.

The eldest of five siblings herself, it was Cynthia's job to tend to the younger ones when her mother was gone. Her schooling didn't even begin until about the fifth grade when a case worker for the Department of Public Welfare found her foraging for food in the neighborhood alleyways, thus revealing her pathetic existence. At age 13 she had her first child, never sure of who the father was. As she spoke, she tried not to smile for her teeth were rotting very badly and some had fallen out.

Cynthia was one of the most timid persons I have ever known. Seldom did she raise her eyes when talking to you. She knew virtually nothing beyond the four-square-block area where she had been born and lived her life. She was illiterate and ignorant about so many things. She knew nothing of her entitlements as a person, much less as an American.

She did not know where welfare or food stamps came from. She was often filled with fear, so when she encountered anyone in authority, she was always afraid that she might say something that would cause her meager benefits to be terminated.

Cynthia and so many like her—the very poor—would never have the personal confidence or knowledge to understand and pursue social benefits for herself or her children. She did not know of networks that might help.

Only strong local, state, and federal support systems might, with immense and consistent hard work, pull people like Cynthia out of this disempowering poverty and restore them to sufficient strength and will to get appropriate help. But such systems, as we all know, do not exist. What does exist is a system of overworked, understaffed, and underpaid welfare workers.

This inadequate social welfare system, coupled with the permanently debilitating nature of this kind of poverty, makes fools of those wealthier citizens who assume that all poor people are equally capable of participation in programs meant to change their lives. Tragically, there is little understanding that there exists an American caste system with the very, very poor clinging to the bottom rung of that system's ladder with no viable way out.

Cynthia died of pneumonia and deprivation at age 25. Two of her seven children preceded her in death.

During the 60s and 70s, many of us were engaged, we thought, in crushing forever racial prejudice and injustice. Our marches, protests, legislation, and writings were all so aimed. We were convinced in the end that we had made substantial progress and so we rested. We neglected to understand that there were others exhaling their breath of hate on a new generation that was breathing it in. Thus, we learned that if the war were to be won, we could never leave the battlefield. The racial war and its direct and collateral damage continue to rage. Following is a selection of short stories describing such damage.

THE ENDLESS WAR

I **was working in the inner-city schools of Chicago.** One afternoon I was in the library talking with a group of middle school children. We talked for over an hour. One of the girls seemed intensely focused upon me. When we finished I said to her, "You seemed to be watching me very closely." She smiled and said, "I was." She then added, "I've never seen a white man in the real, just on television. I'm so glad you're nice."

The first graders from three inner city schools screamed with delight as their field trip busses were approaching downtown Chicago. I asked, "Is downtown that exciting?" Dr. Phedonia Johnson, Director of CANAL, the Chicago desegregation project replied, "No, it's not downtown Chicago that has them so excited. You see, Ray, the neighborhoods that they live in are dominated by rival gangs, so if these young children leave their neighborhoods, they are not safe. They were excited because they were looking at the trees lining these downtown Chicago streets. Many of them had never seen living trees before."

My wife and I had been at a party for teachers. When we left, rather than going home we went to a restaurant /bar near Chicago that we understood was often frequented by teachers. We went with a teacher friend named Otto who taught English literature. We were sitting and enjoying one another's company when a stranger came up behind Otto and whispered something we couldn't hear. Otto excused himself and left with the stranger. I became uneasy. I asked myself, "Who would Otto know in this area of Chicago?"

I told Marion that I was going to look for him and asked her to wait. At the back of the restaurant area near a dance floor not then in use, I saw Otto surrounded by seven or eight white men. I approached and asked, "Everything all right?" One of the larger men turned to me and said, "You the one who brought this N***** in here?" I glanced at Otto who appeared terrified. I responded, "Yes, we are teachers." He replied, "Not very bright teachers, are ya?" As he spoke, he began punching me in the chest with his right closed fist—hard enough to cause me to continue to fall back.

He said, "you're a N***** lover, aren't ya?'" I did not raise my fists or act in any aggressive manner. I could see in Otto's eyes a plea for my restraint. The other men slowly followed, laughing and jeering as they did. Eventually, they pushed both Otto and me out into the street with a warning. I found Marion and we all left.

Marion and I thought about that incident for a long time. We reflected on the humiliation of our friend Otto, the fear we felt, the unfairness of it all. We knew that while we had escaped physical brutality that night, we had not escaped the ugliness borne out of ignorance and hate.

Don Sims, a Native American Chief, was the administrative head of Riverside Indian School in Oklahoma. Over the years we had become close friends. Don's never ending commitment was to find ways to instill pride in Native American children.

GAAGII

One of Don's most prized projects, designed to instill pride in his students, was the one he worked out with *USA Today*. He arranged for each pupil—450 plus—to receive that paper every day. These students would find on the address bar their name, identifying them as the paper's intended recipient. Afterwards, walking through Don's campus was a real pleasure as one could observe young men and women sitting in their favorite corner quietly reading. It is for me a very special memory.

Sadly, this uniquely empowering experience which had brought such pleasure would eventually result in profound shame for one of these proud students. It was mid-January when Don asked me to come to Riverside. I got there and went immediately to his office. His normal demeanor of strength and optimism had faded. He asked me to sit and then slowly told me a story that one of his 14-year-old Navajo students, Gaagii Nez, had shared with him.

Gaagii related to Don that he had never been as proud as when he received his *USA Today* newspaper. His name was on the paper—not handwritten but actually printed in the address bar. He had never before seen his name in print. He saved the paper to take to his grandfather Niyoi, Chief of his tribe in Arizona. They would look at it together, this first of his newspapers, and both would be proud.

It would not be until December that he would take the bus ride From Oklahoma to Arizona and his home. There was a stop in

Flagstaff and he got off. He needed to use the bathroom. As he left the bus, he carried only his treasured newspaper.

No sooner had he finished going to the bathroom and washing his hands when two big white men came in. The bigger of the two looked down at Gaagii and said, "Hey, Indian, gimme that G**damn newspaper." Gaagii told Don that he grasped his paper tight, looked up nervously and replied, "It is mine." "Give it here, Indian. Probably can't read anyway." Then both men laughed. Gaagii told Don that he sensed danger and tried to run and escape but they were too big and blocked his way. In the brief fight that ensued, his newspaper was shredded. As he lay on the bathroom floor he could hear the men as they left, "Damn paper isn't even today's."

He then crawled to the urinal where parts of his newspaper lay. He found the label with his name and picked it up. It was stained with urine and getting wet now from his own tears falling quietly from his face. He felt such shame. How would he tell Niyoi?

Don looked up, tears now streaming slowly down his face. "Why, Ray, why?"

I could think of nothing that would provide comfort, so we just sat there together in the silence of his office.

During the Great Depression, many women in the poverty communities of America did house work for the families of means. The homes of these wealthy families were in more affluent neighborhoods. Most of these affluent neighborhoods were some distance from the neighborhoods of the poor. To get to work a woman had normally only two options. Take a bus that would cost her five cents each way, or walk. The option that was always taken despite the weather or how well she felt was to walk. Walking saved her a dime and a dime was the price of a loaf of bread. The shortest path of that walk, regardless of where she lived, in this country, was normally along a railroad track. Once the track approached the affluent neighborhood she would leave the tracks and head to the house where she was employed.

THE CHRISTMAS PURSE

House cleaning work was sought after. Although it paid only about 15 cents per hour, an average week's pay of approximately $3.00 paid for a family's weekly food and sometimes also for a pair of shoes or such. Most men at that time were unemployed, so the house work money of the mother and daughters, if a household had a daughter who could also work, provided the primary and often only source of family income.

The date was Friday, December 21, 1934, three days before the Polish Wigilia (the Christmas Eve traditional meal). It was 6:15 p.m. and the temperature outside was 12 degrees above zero. In addition, it was very windy. Ma Golarz was very late coming home from work. Pa and her two older sons Walt and Lefty were getting very nervous. On Fridays she was normally home by 4:30 p.m. Lefty was getting dressed to go out and look for her.

At that moment there was heavy pounding at the back door. The door then swung open and Ma, tripping on the top entry way stair, fell into the kitchen with a horrendous thud. As she fell, Lefty and Walt were immediately at her side. Pa and their younger sister Anne came rushing from the living room. As they lifted her, they could feel that her hands were icy cold and bleeding. Further, blood was running down the front of both legs from her knees that were badly scratched, bruised, and dirty. She had somewhere lost her head scarf and her hair was in a total state of disarray, her face beet-red and dirty. She looked up, crying. At that moment, Pa gently lifted her into his arms and said quietly and gently, "Mary, Mary." He held her there for a while in the kitchen, then carried her to a comfortable place in the living room.

When she finally calmed a bit, they asked her what had happened.

She explained that on the way home she lost her change purse—the little black one with embroidered blue and green flowers. The change purse contained this week's wages of $3.70, her Christmas Eve meal money. She said she knew she had the purse when she was on the tracks because just before then she had used her handkerchief to wipe her face and the change purse was in her coat pocket. When she was still on the tracks, but nearer home, she felt for it and it was gone. She said then that she searched and searched, often on her hands and knees, but she couldn't find it. Then it was getting dark so she came home to get a flashlight. She then wept.

Lefty, visibly shaken, looked at his mother and said, "Don't worry, Ma, we'll find it." Then to Walt, he asked, "Ready?"

Walt responded, "Let's go. Get a flashlight and a lantern."

As they walked towards the tracks, Lefty and Walt stopped at Kal's house to let him know that they wouldn't be home and could, therefore, not get together with him as planned. They also told him what they were about and then proceeded to the tracks where it was cold, quite windy, and dark. They started with the location where Ma told them she first felt the purse gone. Then slowly, with their flashlight and lantern turned on, they walked her route northwest to where she would have started to walk the tracks. They walked slowly but found nothing.

It was now near 8:30 p.m., the wind was picking up and the temperature was dropping. They turned back and began to retrace their steps—now a little less confident.

As they walked back, they could see that they were approaching several lights of unknown origin in the distance. As they got closer, they could hear feint talking from the location of the lights that now seemed to be moving toward them. They then heard a shout from a voice they immediately recognized to be Kal Borbely's.

Kal spoke, "Hey, what you two guys doin' on the tracks? Looking to steal coal?"

Lefty answered, "That you, Kal?"

Kal replied, "Who the hell do you think it is—an early Santa Claus with a bunch of elves?"

By this time, they were coming upon the group of nine to ten of their semi-pro football teammates. Walt yelled out, "What are all you guys doin' out here?"

Johnny Gorski jokingly responded, "We heard that the last engineer who came racing through here shook his train and there are coins all over the damn tracks. Hi ya, Walt."

Walt said, "Thanks for coming, Johnny."

Johnny replied, "Hey, bunch of us were just sittin' around a warm fire at Wusic's gas station just gettin' fat and needin' a brisk walk outdoors when Kal told us about your Ma's purse. So, what can we do?"

Walt said, "Well, how about if we all stay together, spread out along the track, and slowly walk the whole distance Ma walked back and forth until we find it."

Gorski agreed, "That's as good a plan as any. Let's do it."

For the next three hours on that cold and windy night, the teammates searched along the track for the little flowered purse. Back and forth. Back and forth. Back and forth. It was now nearing midnight when behind Walt and Lefty, who were in the lead along the track, Gorski exclaimed, "We found it."

Walt and Lefty turned and raced back to where Gorski was standing. Everyone gathered around as Gorski with both of his hands overlapped and cupped together held a pile of coins, mostly dimes, nickels, and pennies. As Lefty and Walt stood dumbstruck looking at his hands with this pile of money, Johnny Gorski said, "It's $3.61. Somewhere nine cents fell out of your Ma's purse."

Walt shaking his head slowly looked up into Johnny's eyes and said, "Johnny, we can't take this money from you guys."

Johnny simply said, "We aren't givin' it to you and Lefty. It's for a little old Polish lady, sitting and praying in your living room that her sons are gonna find her purse with her Christmas meal money like they promised they would."

Lefty just stood there trembling, his arms down at his sides. He was psychologically defenseless. As he looked at Johnny and the others, it was clear that he was having trouble holding it together. He took a deep breath, swallowed, and shaking his head, just looked at his friends, this band of teammates. Though he tried, he wasn't completely successful in holding back the tears.

At close to 1:00 a.m. that morning, Ma got her $3.61. She knew it wasn't hers because she had three dollar bills, two quarters, and two dimes in her change purse. But they made her take it. She was never told who specifically was out there that night, but from that day, whenever any of her son's teammates were in the house, there was a small pot of coffee percolating on the stove.

The little change purse was never found.

In a "Christmas Carol" by Charles Dickens the image of two children are shown to Scrooge. The spirit reveals to Scrooge, "This boy is ignorance, this girl want. Beware them both but most of all beware this boy for on his brow I see that written which is doom, unless the writing is erased."

CITIZEN'S DRUM

D uring my military service I had an instructor whose daily end-of-class challenge still resounds: "What will you read today to help you remain an informed citizen of this American democracy. How will you hear, as clearly as you can the sound of the citizen's drum?" In my youth I did not understand the depth of his meaning. But his passionate delivery provoked a continual, lifelong reflection. Lately I pondered. When had I first heard the sound of the citizen's drum? And who beat that drum for me?

My reflections took me back to WWII when I sat on a kitchen chair with my child's feet dangling as I watched my immigrant grandmother reading her treasured newspapers. In her broken English she would read to me of things I did not understand. What I did understand was her love of those newspapers, the likes of which were often prohibited in her native country. Though her English was imperfect, her reading was intense and reflected a passion to know. She provided for me my first encounter with the sound of the citizen's drum. I was learning of the power and the need to be informed.

As a high school student I took composition. One assignment I was given was to write a paper that developed an argument. Several days after turning it in, Miss Virden pulled me aside. She said, "This is a nice start. Now find authoritative sources that challenge your position. It is easy to create a position if you have not read and, thus, not heard the argument of those who disagree." My internship in citizenship was continuing. I was being taught to listen to the various sounds of the drum. In college the beat continued. Careful writing of anything serious was simply expected as was the inclusion of significant related research.

For most of the twentieth century we were either at war or poised and ready to defend our way of life—democracy. Many to this end gave their lives. Others returned home forever wounded. Today, whether we are a democracy, autocracy, or dictatorship has become for many people no more than a subject for academic discourse. And sadly many of our fellow Americans have become complacent and ignorant.

Multiple sources report that merely a third of our citizens see democracy as essential and preferred. Only half of those graduating college will ever again in their lifetime read a book, and only half of those will read to be informed. In a national election less than 60% are likely to take the time to vote. Many fellow Americans have, through such complacency, become the ignorant "Eloi" of H.G.Well's *Time Machine*, thus increasing their vulnerability to the "Morlocks" of today.

David Brooks in a *New York Times* OP-ED painted an even darker picture. "At the dawn of the internet, people hoped free communication would lead to an epoch of peace, understanding and democratic communication. Instead, we're seeing polarization, alternative information universes and the rise of autocracy."

Like those of my vintage, mornings I pour my coffee and spread out local and New York papers with my wife. Most times we surf a muted TV, moving from news service to news service. Evenings we often sit with various informative magazines and books and enjoy discussions provoked by such. I have heard the sound of the drum too long to ignore it now. Like my immigrant grandmother the quest to remain informed has become too important.

Years ago I taught government. If I were teaching today, I would attempt to convince this new generation of their obligation to become meaningfully knowledgeable—to treasure the sound of the citizen's drum. Remaining ignorant cannot be a choice. Ignorance will, in time, inevitably snatch from these citizens their irreplaceable inheritance—democracy itself.

His name was Tom. He was a student in my government class. He possessed a provocative depth of inquiry not found in most his age.

A Christmas Card

On a cold, Friday afternoon in February we were studying the disparity of wealth existing among nations. I could see that Tom was thinking intensely about the topic, yet he did not participate. He said nothing. Finally, I said to him, "Tom, what are you thinking?" He looked up and somewhat apologetically said, "I'd rather not say." I gently persisted. Tom then answered. His response was neither adversarial nor challenging.

He simply said, "Mr. Golarz, there's no morality in the world." His response was clearly not cognitive, but rather a response that seemed to come from someplace deep inside of his soul. Had it been a cognitive response, I would have debated. But his response was clearly more in the manner of a core value. So I simply said, "Tom, I disagree." Soon class was over. I sat in the faculty lounge lamenting that I did not have the skill to dissuade him of his position. I felt, as teachers often do, that I had failed him. Where was the magic of wisdom?

Several weeks later there was a scheduled exam. Three students, including Tom, missed the exam. Tom's absence was for a reason that did not require my permitting a makeup exam. Several days later, as students were leaving class, I asked Tom to wait. When we were alone, I said, "Tom, I'll be in the building late tomorrow. If you would like to come by and make up the exam, I'll be here." He looked surprised and said, "That's awfully nice of you, Mr. Golarz."

The next thing I said I hadn't planned. My response came from somewhere other than myself. I said, "Tom, it's simply the moral thing to do." He looked stunned. I continued, "Will you be there?" After a long moment he said quietly and slowly, "Yes, sir. I'll be there."

Tom took his exam. We never discussed my comment. Several months later he graduated. Six months after graduation, I received a phone call near midnight, "Mr. Golarz, this is Tom. Do you think we could have coffee and talk?" A half hour later we met at George's Diner in East Chicago. We drank coffee and talked all night. At 7:00 a.m., I shaved in the faculty lounge and went to my classroom to teach. Later, Tom and I met again, and again we talked most of the night. Soon thereafter we lost contact. I learned years later that he had been severely wounded in military action and decorated for valor.

I heard no more of Tom until recently. My wife Marion usually opens our Christmas cards. One evening while reading the cards she asked, "Who's Tom?" At first I didn't remember, but then I realized that "Tom" was the former student I had shared those long conversations with so many years ago.

He wrote, "This Christmas thank-you note is long overdue. I'm an engineer in California now and many evenings I coach basketball for wheelchair-handicapped kids. One of my kids struggles emotionally and wanted to give up. Recently he asked me, "Coach, why do you give me so many chances?" I wanted to tell him that it was "simply the moral thing to do," but I'm not sure he would have understood. I know, however, that you will understand. So thanks, Mr. Golarz."

I treasure that card as only teachers do. We hear too infrequently that we made a difference, but differences are made by teachers every day. No teacher should ever forget that.

One of my administrative assignments was to oversee the dropout problem. The school district had nearly 23,000 students. Annually we lost nearly 500. Despite our efforts only about 200 returned. We would then rent an old, vacant, downtown storefront facility and employ specialized staff. Within a month, a full 70% of those returning would again drop out. Large school districts throughout our country were experiencing the same thing. Our lack of success was frustrating.

BELIEVE IN ME

At a conference in Phoenix, Dr. Gary Phillips explained that some years earlier this national problem of reoccurring dropouts did not occur in Seattle for a span of several years. Returning dropouts were staying at an 80% level. He explained further. The Seattle public schools had not been able to find a suitable downtown facility for returning dropouts, so contractual arrangements were made with the University of Washington to rent several of their classrooms.

Soon neighbors of these dropouts throughout the city were asking of the dropouts, "Where are you going with those books? Thought you had dropped out of school." The returning students proudly replied, "My classes are at the University of Washington now." What had Seattle inadvertently tied into? What serendipity?

Sometime later I was presenting at a conference in Tulsa regarding the power of belief systems. At the break, one of Tulsa's assistant superintendents asked to share a story. When we resumed she began. As a young teacher of special education at the elementary school level, she challenged her students to believe in themselves. She told them to dream, for only through challenging dreams could they succeed.

After school one of her mildly mentally handicapped special education students, a little girl, timidly came to her. "Teacher, I have a dream, but I'm afraid." "Why, child, are you afraid?" "I'm not smart like other children, so my dream is foolish." "Never say that. Tell me about your dream, and I will help you." The young child then said, "I want to win the school spelling bee." The assistant superintendent shared with us the terror she felt. Had she set this beautiful child up for failure—this child whose eyes and heart were now filled with hope? How could she tell this child that her dream was not attainable? She couldn't.

For the next nine weeks every day after school and on weekends, she dedicated herself to assisting this child and her mother in preparing for the contest, all the while convinced that failure and tragedy were looming. The night before the competition she confessed to us that she did not sleep.

Then came the competition. The final round of the competition was the most difficult for her to watch. Would it—could it really happen? Then the miracle occurred. The child with an impossible dream won, and from this little girl she heard, "I won because I knew that you knew that I could. I knew it in my heart." Weeks later at the city competition, she didn't get eliminated until the fifth round.

Years ago, Charles Horton Cooley created a concept titled "The Looking Glass Self." Fundamentally, the concept suggests that *who I am* is a combination of *who I think I am*, *who you think I am*, and *who I think you think I am*. Much of the essence of a child's identity rests with us. Do they believe that we believe in them? How do they know? Do we house them in an old, vacant, downtown storefront, or in an edifice that is elegant and gives them a feeling of dignity?

Do we fail to inspire them, or do we empower them by showing them how to chase after their dreams?

Children become the manifestation of the dreams that they believe we dream with them before they dream of succeeding in the dreams of their own.

I was serving as the school superintendent. A group of teachers approached me and requested that they, along with parents, be permitted to create the first public charter school in Indiana.

CAN YOU HELP US CREATE?

T heir enthusiasm had nothing to do with challenging the effectiveness of the current system. Rather, they believed that an alternative school might enhance what we could offer to a community with differing needs and interests. I, along with a visionary school board, agreed to support their effort. We then backed away and let them design their school, allowing and encouraging their artistic design to unfold. Three years later, Discovery School opened with an enrollment of 160 and a waiting list of nearly 90.

This school was established without incurring any financial burden to the district. It was enthusiastically supported by the teachers union and teachers throughout the district, and it remained under the umbrella of the existing district. Parents and community members had been involved in its design and mission.

Most importantly, this school was not viewed as a competitor for students. Nor was it viewed as being better than the existing schools. It was viewed simply as a different way to respond to the unique needs and interests of a significant number of community parents and their children.

Some years later, a coalition of professional educators came to my home in Bloomington and met with me and teachers from that Discovery School. They asked how best to proceed with a state-wide charter school system. I offered the following advice: First, never create a state-wide system. Only local teachers and parents should initiate and develop such schools. The process should never be the result of a top-down plan designed by a school board, administration, or legislative body. Top-down ventures rarely have the ownership or creativity needed for success. Second, if this school causes an additional cost to the district, then its existence will create anger and resentment within the broader community. Additional cost is, therefore, not an option. Third, the school must have extensive support from the broader community of teachers and parents.

These guidelines were virtually ignored. Instead, government officials and special interest groups such as The American Legislative Executive Council (ALEC) became deeply involved, distorted the charter concept, and created legislation with adversarial intent. The legislation had at its core the premise that American public education had failed. The charter school's evolving implementation predictably created deep divisions within the American community.

As I had warned, we now see and hear at the local level everywhere, angry and hateful discourse among well-intentioned, good people on both sides as they argue over the legality, character, and value of charter schools vs. the local public schools. Sadly, children and teachers in these environments are caught up in this cross-fire and have become collateral damage as they are often confused and worried about the educational choices that have been made for them.

There is only one way to resolve this destructive environment. This can only happen with the removal of the legislators responsible for enacting the laws and procedures which establish and protect charter schools in this deliberately distorted form.

Once this is accomplished, newly elected legislators must reverse the actions that have turned our communities into battlegrounds. We can then once again support our public schools and the teachers who have the willingness to find ways to enhance learning for all of our children. Our salvation so far is that our teachers, our classroom artists, have not left us. Despite the wars being waged, they wait patiently for the time when they can again walk into a superintendent's office and ask, "Can you help us create?"

But don't make them wait too long for even they can run out of patience.

He was a coal miner from southern Indiana and he played a mean bass. He worked in the mines, studied nights, and played in a jazz band. Eventually he went to college and secured a doctorate at Ball State University. His name was Gary Phillips.

Profound Complexity

I met him while he was consulting for the Kettering/Lilly Foundations. This was during the time that Dean Evans served as the Indiana State Superintendent. In addition to Gary's many accomplishments, he was a gifted keynote speaker. Years ago, he gave a keynote address to the school administrators and many teachers of the Chicago Public Schools. From my notes and from my memory of that event, I describe his address below.

First, he started talking about a high school he knew well, telling about an early morning incident that had taken place in the school parking lot. The principal had turned away a carload of armed white adults intent on entering the school to harm several black students. Gary told about a second incident where immediately after school two girls who were in a bathroom were forced to give all of their cash to several older, stronger girls. One girl resisted. Then she was struck in the face and forced to take off all of her clothing. When found, she was hysterical.

He finally told about a junior boy who, on the same day, threatened to kill a teacher. The following morning the police searched him as he attempted to enter the building and removed a loaded revolver from his jacket pocket. Gary completed his description of the school with additional stories in the same vein. When he finished, the audience of some 1500 conference participants was quiet and sober.

He then told his audience about a second high school. He described the school salutatorian, a young woman, captain of her soccer team, who had recently accepted a full academic scholarship to Columbia University. He added that an additional four top scholars of the senior class had also accepted full academic scholarships to other Ivy League schools. He continued to note outstanding student achievements: the chess club taking third place in a national tournament, the band finishing second in a state competition, the girls basketball team winning first place in their division for the third consecutive year. For the next ten minutes, he continued to share stories regarding the accomplishments of many other talented and committed students. When he finished he asked. "Which school would you want your son or daughter to attend?" The answer was so obvious most in the audience, perplexed, sat quietly.

Then Gary continued, "The answer is not so simple or apparent, for what I did not tell you was that the first school and the second school are actually the same school, and all of the incidents that I have described took place in that same school.

It is a school of academic excellence, a school of profoundly difficult problems, a school of winning moments, and of moments that occasionally border on disaster. It is a school that can become better, and a school that must become better. It is, in many respects, the school in your own community. It is, as are all schools, a school that defies a simple grade of A, B, C, D, or F. It is too complex to be judged so simplistically. Like all schools, it is a changing, living, breathing entity that good teachers, committed students, parents, and dedicated principals everywhere try to make better every day.

Don't devalue it by trying to assign some simple label or grade to it. Rather, recognize it as the profound complexity that it is. Then cherish and support it."

In the movie Ben Hur, Drusus, aide to Messala, accompanies the jailer to the cell of Ben Hur's mother and sister. He inquires at the iron cell door, "If you never go into their cell, how is it you know they're still alive?" The jailor replies, "The food disappears."

"The Food Disappears"

When I became superintendent of schools I was sought after, invited to important community meetings, asked to speak, and complimented on my new ideas for change. At one of the grand meetings held for me, I met a woman who was introduced to me as one of our high school teachers. I recall asking her how she liked my new ideas for the district. She replied, "Forgive me. You are my fifth superintendent. If you really want my opinion, visit my classroom." Several weeks later I did.

I found to my surprise that over the past 20 years she had created in her classroom one of the most exciting remedial reading labs I had ever seen outside of fine universities. She had done it all with her own money. Most tragically, I found that I was the only administrator besides her principal to visit her classroom in those 20 years. I asked her to take part with me in the next month's radio program that highlighted special school programs. She agreed on the condition that she could bring some of her students. The program done by her and her students was captivating and extremely professional. More importantly, it also affirmed her worth and dignity.

The following week I visited many classrooms. Everywhere I went I found enthusiastic and exciting teaching. I was so impressed that I began to write simple short thank-you notes acknowledging the moving and professional teaching I had seen. A week or so later a second grade teacher came to my office. She said through her tears, "You sent me a note. I've been teaching for 23 years and no one has ever sent me a note like that before. I have it framed and it hangs behind my desk for all of my children to see." We sat late in my office that afternoon and talked of stars and smiley faces.

The author Peter Drucker asks us to consider the following questions when judging any organization's potential for greatness. I paraphrase: "Do those who work there feel treated with respect and dignity and can they take pride in knowing that someone noticed with admiration what they did?"

Through these teachers I began to understand that my new ideas were not the most important ideas. I saw that my true significance and the true significance of all of the organizational leaders would be found in our capacity to honor and recognize all of those who quietly work daily with little reward or recognition. The organization's potential for greatness is in our hands—not because of the initiation of new ideas, programs, or technologies created at the top of our bureaucracies, but because we know and can articulately speak of the work already being done by our teachers.

To be a truly great school district, our commitment to and support of those who daily serve must go far beyond our knowing simply that "the food disappears."

Except for Native Americans we have always been a nation of immigrants. We bring from our various foreign countries our dreams and our willingness to work. Do not fear us for we are you. Simply give us enough room to stand and in one generation we will strengthen the whole.

WHERE DREAMS CAN COME TRUE

His name was Joseph. He was just 14 when he left his home in the village of Zagorz, located in a part of Poland known as Galicia. Over many centuries and at various times, the boundaries of this section of Poland had shifted as neighboring countries alternately claimed that this land belonged to them. Thus, the authentic citizenship of the people who were born and lived in this region was often unclear. Some people claimed their heritage to be Ukraine, others to be Austrian. Still others claimed to be Polish. Joseph considered himself to be Polish.

When he left his home, he had with him only one change of clothing and a book of Polish hymns given to him by his father. He joined the millions of other Polish immigrants who were leaving their homeland to go to America. Like immigrants who came from countries all over the world, they were looking to escape poverty, oppression, foreign domination, and the ever-present threat of war. Their dream was to provide a better life for themselves and their families.

Once here, Joseph would meet Mary Kot, also a Polish immigrant. They would marry and eventually have five children. Joseph was full of hope that he and his family would become educated, economically secure, and able to participate in this democracy as full-fledged citizens. He was more than willing to work very hard to fulfill these dreams. He had no idea, however, just how hard life could become in this country.

Over the next 20 years he would face profound hardships. While he labored in the steel mills, he and his family lived in company housing. These accommodations were limited to one room with a single light bulb hanging from the ceiling. Joseph and Mary hung a sheet to separate the sleeping area from the living area. Furniture was at a minimum. Barely able to provide food for his family, Joseph marched in the 1919 national steel strike where he was fired upon by his own, local police. While he was not injured, friends were killed and he assisted in their burial. As difficult as all of this was, he persisted in his efforts to make America his home.

In 1930, his second son John, an eighth-grade student at St. Mary's school, was awarded a trophy in honor of his academic achievement. Joseph was pleased. One of the reasons for his coming to America was being fulfilled. However, great difficulties still lay ahead, for in 1932 as a consequence of the Great Depression, he would be laid off and lose the house that he had built with the help of his friends. In 1935, at the height of the depression, his youngest son Andrew was suffering from diet deficiencies and had become so weak he needed special medical attention. Only through the assistance of the General Relief Agency would Joseph's family be given the $13.00 needed to pay for such medical attention. Assistance from that General Relief Agency would later provide food. These interventions were life-saving.

For a while things got easier. But then the United States entered into the war that was raging in Europe. In 1942, Andrew, the son who needed medical care as a child, enlisted in the United States Army along with other young Americans, many of whom were also the children of immigrants. On June 6, 1944, Andrew and his comrades participated in the assault on Omaha Beach in Normandy. Andrew would be among the soldiers who were fortunate enough to survive. At war's end he would come home, marry, and become godfather to his brother's eldest son. He became a policeman and rose to the rank of captain in the same police department whose members had, in 1919, fired upon and killed fleeing steelworkers.

Andrew's godson—this book's author—would eventually find his way to Indiana University where he secured his post-graduate degrees. Early in his career as an administrator, he was appointed to the position of Executive Director of the General Referral Agency of the Hammond Public Schools where for many years he would oversee the dispensing of monies to the poor—the same General Relief Agency that had given the life-saving assistance to his godfather Andrew in 1935.

Another of Joseph's grandsons would become the executive administrator responsible for employee-labor relations in that same plant where police and hired men shot and killed so many immigrant workers in the 1919 carnage. As Joseph had dreamed, his family was participating in the opportunities and challenges citizenship presented.

Joseph did not live long enough to see the continuing success and contributions his descendants achieved. One of his great granddaughters performed at Lincoln Center and another became an accomplished writer. He did not live to see one of his great grandsons play in the Rose bowl, nor another go to Africa to teach mathematics to the children of the poor, nor another receive the Bronze Star for performing surgery under fire as an American doctor in Iraq, nor another rise to the position of senior vice-president of a prestigious American firm.

Immigrants and their descendants have forever been a significant part of the cement that binds this great nation together. Joseph's story is only one of the millions of stories that tell the truth about the bright, productive, and very brave souls who have come to us from countries across this world. They have not been the burden on our schools and other institutions as some would have us believe.

On the contrary, they have risen to the levels of extraordinary success as teachers, students, soldiers, doctors, artists, and talented workers in all walks of life. With determination and sacrifice, they have earned and honored their citizenship.

Without them we would be less than the great people that we are.

It's 5:45 in the morning and still dark. Jack, a seven-year veteran, fully certified and licensed math teacher, is already awake. Lying in bed in his room at the Cross-Town Hotel, he is waiting for the phone to ring. The call will come soon advising him which school he needs to report to this morning. He no longer has a permanent school assignment.

No Place for Jack

The phone rings and he answers, "Yes, this is Jack. Yes, I know where it is. You have a nice day too."

Struck out again. It's the notorious Jackson Middle School, not particularly kind to substitute teachers and a fifty-minute drive from his location, But, no time to lament—just dress, grab a quick cup of coffee, a donut, and hit the road.

As he approaches the interstate, it's clear that there must be an accident up ahead, for it looks like a parking lot as far as he can see. While waiting for traffic to move, he begins to reflect: "How did this happen to me? Got my degree in math twelve years ago, banged around a few places, even taught overseas, and for the last seven years taught calculus and pre-calculus right here in this district. Students in my last assignment voted me teacher of the year. So what did I do wrong? Why am I floating around the district without an assignment?"

Moving again, Jack began to think about when things changed drastically. He knew that this district, like so many other urban school centers, had restructured their schools and replaced them with alternative schools like magnets and charters. But, could this explain why there were hundreds of surplus teachers without a specific assignment?

Then he thought about what happened right before school began. There must have been 300 of us there—all District Three teachers—all still unassigned: math, physics, English teachers, twenty-and thirty-year veterans, and much younger folks like me. He remembered clearly what was said. "Ladies and Gentlemen: There are teaching vacancies in the district. Most of your former schools are now charters. Some are magnets. So, since you weren't kept by these schools, you will need to check the list of vacancies each morning on your computers, arrange for interviews, and secure one of the available vacancies."

Jack had followed these directions. He had fourteen interviews and no fewer than 45 administrators had advised him by phone or during his personal visits to their buildings that the vacancies listed on the district's master list were inaccurate. "There are no math vacancies here, never were, or they were filled last week," he was told repeatedly.

Jack continued to ponder. Principals control their own budgets now. Do all the surplus teachers who were at the late August meeting simply cost too much? Could it be that simple, that calculated? The meeting I attended was for teachers in District Three. There are four other districts, and each of them had a similar meeting. Are we looking at nearly 2,000 displaced, licensed, viable teachers? Is this phenomenon only occurring here, or is it also happening in other huge school systems like New York, San Francisco, Philadelphia, and Miami Dade County?

Jack finally arrives at Jackson Middle School. I hope I get a classroom assignment today, preferably in math. Last week four of my five days I had no classroom assignment. So I usually stayed in the teachers' lounge, except for last Wednesday when I volunteered to help the custodian move books.

After school, Jack went to the central office personnel department again just to check on his file. He was told, "No, Jack, there's nothing negative in your personnel file. As a matter of fact, there isn't much in your file at all." Jack left the office more confused and discouraged than ever. Maybe, he thought to himself, I just need to get out of teaching.

That spring he reluctantly did. As he drove away, his Starbucks coffee spilled on his framed teacher of the year award lying on the passenger front seat. He watched as the coffee seeped under the glass. He wondered why he didn't try to stop it.

I did my student teaching at Hammond Technical Vocational High School. One day the principal, Mr. Wilson, invited me to lunch in his office.

ARTISTRY

I n his office was a large bookcase filled with black bound volumes. Each volume identified a subject matter course offered during the Great Depression. He explained, "During those times students would often need to drop out and go to work. Upon returning, they came back to a set of failing grades for courses never completed. Discouraged, they left." He explained further. "In order to remedy this condition we teachers structured all of our courses with content sections. Thus, if students had to drop out, they were given a report card showing the number of sections completed and the number remaining for each course. Upon returning to school, they would simply finish the remaining sections. Failure would not occur again for the children of depression-era poverty."

I asked, "Why did you stop?" He replied, "The state declared that our strategy was somehow violating their standards. I keep these volumes to remind myself of an earlier, more flexible and empathetic time."

I received a phone call from a superintendent in Illinois. He called to inquire about our school district's very successful kindergarten intervention program. He suggested that he wanted to send a team of administrators to study our effort, and if the team found it to be a "best practice," they would implement it.

I responded, "Sir, a specific or predesigned model has little to do with the program's success. The creative implementation and on-going modifications are all in the hands of the teachers. The extraordinary success is due to the continuous hard work and creativity of that staff. I hate to see you waste a trip." He responded, "Well then, how do you administratively maintain control?" I said, "You don't, the teachers are in control." We ended our conversation. He never called back.

Artists must control the art. I taught seventh grade history as I was taught: first student, stand and read; second student, stand and read; third student, and so on. My students were not really learning or understanding much history.

One day I said to a student, "Come up to the chalkboard and make a mark at the far left end indicating the arrival of Columbus in 1492. Then, assuming the entire front chalkboard is all of American history up to today, make a mark where you think the signing of the Constitution took place." About three feet from her first mark, she made the second mark. Then I asked her to mark where we are now. She placed this mark at the end of the chalkboard some twenty feet away. Students became curious and engaged. One student suggested that we become more precise allowing one inch for each year of history. When we did, we were all stunned. The period from 1492 to the Constitution filled the entire chalkboard. No one had understood how much time had passed between the arrival of Columbus and the signing of the Constitution. An additional chalkboard was needed to represent history from the Constitution to the present time. In the following weeks, suggestions for added information came quickly—a line for famous persons, another line for inventions, and a line representing population growth. History, in their hands, was becoming alive.

Some years ago, Marion and I were watching *Back stage at Lincoln Center* on PBS. Zubin Mehta was being interviewed with respect to the qualities essential for conducting. He spoke of how he watched the artists as they watched him until at some point in the performance they tell him with a knowing look to let go. He does so, and at that point the music becomes their own. He, the conductor, simply holds them together.

Great teaching is a daily creative art. It occurs in environments where the artist feels free and trusted to create. Why would we want it any other way?

Stephen Gould's The Mismeasure of Man opens by presenting a dialogue between Socrates and Glaucon wherein they fabricate a myth. The myth suggests that God had framed people differently—bright people (commanders), average people (auxiliaries), and dull people (husbandmen and craftsmen). Socrates and Glaucon then agree that the Greek citizenry would never believe such an absurd myth. However they speculate, "But their sons may be made to believe, and their son's sons and posterity after them."

WHAT IS INTELLIGENCE?

Are we that posterity? Have we structured our institutions including education to mirror and support the myth?

Early in the twentieth century, a test was created called the Stanford-Binet. Over time it became viewed as the definitive measure of human intelligence, even though this was not the designer's original intent. The test, administered individually, became the standard by which other intelligence tests were judged. But does the Binet or any of the other "intelligence" tests really measure intelligence?

Although test results highly correlate with proficiencies in math and language arts, the results do not also correlate highly with empathy, civility, musical skills, or artistic capacities—capacities which also reflect intelligence. Might all of these tests simply be measuring academic achievement—academic achievement that we all know is tied to wealth and opportunity?

Beginning in the 1980s, researchers like Howard Gartner in his *Frames of Mind*, and Daniel Goleman in his *Emotional Intelligence*, began to seriously challenge the very narrow kind of intelligence definition being promoted. For a time these researchers had a profound impact on the way intelligence was defined and assessed.

Their work had a significant effect, especially on the way teaching methods were modified to broaden instructional strategies, notably at the primary and secondary levels. Their work also prompted many in the business community to look beyond academic grades in a resume.

Tragically, beginning with the unprecedented move to make our students more competitive with students in other countries, we have reverted to the use of very narrow standardized testing to define what we will accept as evidence of gradations of intelligence. We have come seriously close to accepting the myth that Socrates and Glaucon had proposed and feared would come to be. (1)

As a young teacher, I once taught all seniors whose total class was divided into seven academic competency levels. The entire senior class had been tested using a group intelligence test that highly correlated with math and language art skills. Throughout the day I taught different levels. For example, the first period might consist of a group of level four students and second period might consist of a group of level six students.

My daily teaching experiences clearly were a contradiction to this supposition of gradation. For example, I recall a distraught senior girl who was placed in the level one group, supposedly the smartest group. One day, this senior girl came to me in tears, having failed miserably an essay type exam. The exam had required that she be able to think critically and respond logically to questions over material we had been studying.

"Please, Mr. Golarz, just give me a multiple choice exam. I have everything memorized." In other observations I found many students who possessed proficiencies that contradicted their assigned level. My finest art student, for example, was a level six despite the fact that artistic achievement requires considerable intellectual abilities.

In later years as an administrator, I directed gifted education as well as special education. The one constant observation I made in those years was that many young people had been misplaced and mislabeled. Often children who had been labeled as gifted were simply lost when asked to engage in complex projects. The greatest tragedy, however, was to find children who had lost their capacity to believe in themselves because they had come to believe in the demeaning label placed on them by some paper and pencil test.

Intelligence is never a narrow cognitive thing. Only when we understand and enhance both the discrete skills and the full range of everyone's intellectual potential will we discover and reap the benefits of the gifts that allow us all to attain greatness. There are not preordained commanders, auxiliaries, and craftsmen—there is simply a world filled with a wide diversity of people God has created who possess an array of incredible gifts of differing types and sizes.

Is it not time for us to set the myth aside, for it continues to obstruct our seeing one another properly—of seeing the potential sensitivity, deep understanding, and intuitive thought that exists in us all.

1 Golarz and Golarz, *The Problem Isn't Teachers,* Section Five: The War Over Purpose, pp 138-152.

Evenings, in homes across this great land, children sit at kitchen tables struggling with academic content that their parents and they have been told is essential to know if they are going to score high on standardized tests. The atmosphere in the house is again tense and the momentary respite at day's end, essential to good mental health is gone—preempted by this insanity.

On those same tense evenings, a tired teacher reworks the lesson for tomorrow. Her constant question is, "Will this help with the upcoming standardized test?" Invariably this question is followed by another question, "How long can I continue this?"

THE MADNESS OF TESTING

U sing standardized tests to assess a student's level of achievement is the game of politicians, not of local school boards, teachers, or parents. The lives that American parents and teachers want for children are filled rather with an array of richness and growth in a multitude of areas. Doing well in school is important. But they also want their children to taste, enjoy, and grow from so much more.

They want them to lie in a grassy field on a summer day and read a novel for pleasure, know the sound of Bach, enjoy rap, and share in the caring of an elderly grandparent. They want them to enjoy and be proud of their capacity to manipulate new technologies, play in a football game, run a race, attend a prom, and gain skills with the many tools that they find in their family garage and kitchen.

They want them to take pride in and understand the history of their own race and ethnicity, sense and then respond to the needs of their fellow man, know the thrill of hitting a home run and glory in the skill of controlling a soccer ball, knee-to-knee-to-toe-to-knee. They want them to babysit a neighbor's child and earn their own dollar, have time to reflect on the world's new discoveries, get a little choked up at the playing of their own national anthem, and waste away an afternoon playing basketball with friends in a park.

If this means that some nation with less freedom and less true breadth and depth of knowing outscores them on some artificial measure of greatness, then so be it. These tests measure such a very narrow band of knowing and being. They really measure nothing of the greatness of a people, nor of their potential for greatness.

And if our children find that they need to compete at the highest levels for something that they really want, they will. They always have. Just give them a fair and level competitive field. Then when they come to you, interview them, face-to-face. Never substitute knowing them with a test score. Give them half a fighting chance and they will come the rest of the way.

Throw away your state and national standardized tests. Get back to knowing who these young people really are. All these tests do is obscure their unique value and potential greatness.

I was looking for my American Literature class with a teacher I had never had—Miss May Virden. As I approached, I could see her in the doorway of her classroom greeting students. She appeared to be in her early sixties, no more than four feet, ten inches tall and could not have weighed 90 pounds. Her dress had a high collar and sleeves to the elbows. She held an open book in her hands at waist level; her face had a smile that was warm and compelling.

MISS VIRDEN

She received her bachelor's degree in English from Cornell. She did advanced work at Northwestern. She had been teaching high school literature for nearly 40 years. She brought to each of her classrooms the essence of civility, grace and order.

What I remember most about her classroom was the feeling of relaxation that I experienced. There was no fear that some fellow student might create a disruption or that several students would begin talking during her teaching moments. Her demeanor clearly expressed without words that this was her sacred place, and we were being permitted to participate in a gift that she was creating for us.

One day in mid-January, she announced to us that she had prepared a special treat for us, a treat that had been given to her by one of her professors many years earlier. She had us close our books and asked us to listen attentively. She then began to recite to us, the poem, "The Bells," by Edgar Allan Poe.

Throughout the presentation, we were totally captivated. But our capture was not the result of the words of the poem, rich though they are, but rather by her immersion into the poem: her eyes, the movement of her body, the gestures of her hands, the inflections of her voice, her pitch, her tone at times almost moaning, and the pace of her words both rapid and slow. The bells became real, and we could feel as well as hear and see their many variations. She seemed so alive in that long moment of presentation and then, as quickly as she had started, it was over, and the room grew silent. She had taken us on a journey to a place that we had never been, and in that journey she had introduced us to poetry as we had never known it.

We who attended that high school were the sons and daughters of steelworkers and iron workers. Soot spewing from open-hearth furnaces during the night covered our cars each morning. Most of our grandparents and some of our parents were born in foreign lands. In our homes most of us heard a foreign tongue spoken more frequently than English. We were rough and crass, and we butchered the English language. We butchered it with our Chicago area dialect mixed in with Eastern European idioms and peculiarities as well as with our own street vulgarities. We were as hard an audience as you would ever like to have.

Yet when Miss Virden finished her eloquent delivery, after only a brief silence, we began to applaud. We applauded and applauded, and then began to stand and applaud. We applauded as she stood there before us, and then she nodded and smiled.

It would be years later, only after I had myself become a teacher, that I understood what teachers experience in such rare moments. It's the moment that makes a teacher's journey worthwhile. It is the magical instant of real communication with students that sustains teachers as nothing else does. It is why they stay.

The young boy watched his father kill his mother and then kill himself with a shotgun. He then sat the whole night near the bodies with his four year old brother in his arms. Neighbors found him and his brother the next morning. His name was Jesse and he was only seven years old.

JESSE

I met him as he became a seventh grader. He had just turned 15 and resided at Hoosier Boys Town, a facility for neglected and abused children. I was his teacher and football coach. Though only a year older than most of my players, he was mature beyond his years. He was a handsome young man, tall, wiry and quick. He had the athletic grace that you find normally only in college athletes. I did not know at that time of his tragic early life. Only later would he tell me of it.

We went undefeated in football that season and that was in no small way due to the athletic and leadership skills of Jesse. Oh, he didn't win all of those games by himself. I had a talented group—many also from Hoosier Boys Town. I found with these young men that they would do almost anything for you if they felt that you liked them. I really didn't find it hard to form such meaningful bonds. A dear friend, Dr. Gary Phillips once told me that with abused and neglected children you will often find that they have what he called, "a hole in the soul," and if you could put your hand gently into that hole, they would be your friend forever.

Football season was over and fall was giving way to light winter snows. Our three story school was old. My classroom was on the third floor overlooking the playground below. As a teacher you quickly learn that playground activities reveal many things: the bullies, those isolated or ignored, friendship groups and the various leaders. What you tended not to see too often was the student who, though an acknowledged leader, seemed simply uninterested in his peers. That was Jesse.

He stayed late one afternoon and we talked. I asked him first why he maintained such a social distance from his classmates. His answer was straight forward and simple. "Coach, it's not that I don't like them. I'd simply rather not play with the kids." I lamented at how out of place and alone he must feel.

He then told me of the early childhood tragedy and of his continuing "night monsters." Afterwards we often took walks. He seemed to like that so we walked and talked many times of many things. On one occasion we visited the high school. As we peered into classrooms, it was as if someone had breathed life into him. He was a different kid. My task was clear. If he agreed, we would try to get him to skip eighth grade and move directly into high school. Later, we met with his Boys Town counselor and principal of the high school. We laid out his need to pass the entrance exam. He just sat there, his eyes swelling with tears. Then he said, "I'll pass it." Not long afterwards his counselor called. "Ray, thought you would like to know. He has a flashlight in his bed. Pretty sure he studies most of the night.

Jesse passed that test, graduated high school, fought in Viet Nam, married a wonderful girl, and had two children.

Some years later, as I was walking out of a class I was teaching at Purdue, I heard from behind me, "Hey, coach, want to take a walk?"

On occasion, when I worked in Arkansas, we would drive to one of several elementary schools in the Delta. I always enjoyed such work. Who wouldn't enjoy the trusting simplicity and innocence of these primary children? During these times I had occasion to work with a third grade child named Mary.

LITTLE MARY

Mary was one of seven children. She lived in an old decrepit structure nearly a mile from her school. Her family had a large rain barrel on the side of the structure. This was the family's source of drinking water and water to clean with. In the dry season the river near the house provided such. Life was often times harsh.

The first time I met with Mary was in the fall. Her teacher told me that Mary had virtually no math skills or even a fundamental understanding of math concepts. Thus was my challenge—assist a Mary with math.

Our first conversation went something like this. "I understand that your name is Mary. My name is Mr. G. Would you mind if I help you with your math?" Mary replied, "That's up to you, but ya need to understand it's been tried before." "Well, Mary, can I try?" "Sure, but you got to understand that it's in the blood. My mother and grandmother couldn't do math either—it's in the blood, ya see. Momma told me it's in the blood, but if you want to try, go ahead." My work with Mary on that first day was fruitless except for, I believe, her beginning to like me.

Several weeks later, during the second visit, I got an unanticipated break. As Mary and I were beginning to work, I dropped five or six coins from my pocket as I was attempting to secure a handkerchief. Mary began to pick up the coins and as she did she said, "Can you help me to understand what these mean? All the other kids know what they mean and it's embarrassing for me." I had an opening and

I took it. The various denominations of coins would be my vehicle. For the next several hours we worked slowly and patiently. She was beginning to learn. As we concluded, I said to her, "you're getting to understand this, aren't you?' She smiled and responded, "It could be just one of those things." She wasn't ready to acknowledge that she was beginning to understand.

I would work with Mary several more times. By session's end she could add and subtract using coins nearly as quickly as I could. I said to her, "You're getting to know this, aren't you?" She replied with a sheepish smile, "I have to say yes, Mr. G. cause my momma has told me never to lie, but I don't know math real good yet." I smiled and said, "But you will, Mary, but you will."

Several months later, I received a letter from Mary's teacher. She wanted me to know that Mary had become the math classroom tutor, assisting other children having trouble. She always uses coins as her vehicle to teach. Enclosed in her letter was a note from Mary.

"Mr. G. I am gettin' better and I'm helpin' some other kids. Gettin' them to do the math is the easy part. Gettin' them to believe is harder.

Oh, also, me and my momma went shoppin' and when we got done I told momma how much change she should be gettin' back. On the way home she asked me if I could teach her how to do that. Mr. G, maybe it ain't in the blood –just maybe." Mary

In his early adulthood, Dr Gary Phillips had been a coal miner in Southern Indiana. Later, during his prime, he was one of the most accomplished keynote speakers I have ever known. I am honored to say that he became a close friend. I paraphrase now a story he treasured and told so often in his addresses.

MAURICE

Maurice was a handsome, bright boy. He was born in Canada at the beginning of the Great Depression of the 1930s. In school and at home he was often complimented for his scholarly abilities and his inquisitive mind.

As with virtually all children, his early childhood of exploring and tinkering resulted in some splinters and hammered fingers. At school he also seemed to have little aptitude for "hands- on" endeavors. By third grade the consensus of opinion at home and at school was clear. Maurice is a very bright and inquisitive boy. An academic path to the future is clear. He should, however, avoid that which requires working with his hands.

With such support and clear direction, Maurice walked the academic path, first with exceptional academic success at the high school and undergraduate college levels and then graduate work culminating with his doctorate from Harvard. The academic honors were numerous. After his doctorate, Maurice became a researcher and teacher. He moved from assistant professor to associate professor and, finally, to full professor. He was recognized for his publications and groundbreaking ideas on the nature of human learning. He walked the scholarly path with honor and dignity. Finally, he determined that it was time to retire, enjoy the fruits of his labor, and focus upon his growing grandchildren.

It was in those days of retirement that Maurice found that his most valued moments were taking his grandchildren to the ocean and watching them enjoy the sand and never-ending ocean waves. One of those days as he sat on the beach, his youngest grandson kept bringing to him sticks and ocean soaked pieces of wood. He found one of these wooden gifts quite intriguing. He liked its unfinished but interesting look. Rather than take it home he shoved it under the log upon which he sat. Days later equipped with a pocket knife from his youth he sat on that log and carefully began to whittle that captivating piece of drift wood.

It would take many days, but eventually it began to take the form and shape of what his mind's eye thought it could be. He liked it. He put it in his coat pocket. He took it home. He showed it only to his wife and then placed it on his bedroom dresser—a display for himself alone.

Some months later, one of his house guests, while looking for a bathroom, wandered into his bedroom. He spotted the driftwood piece and was taken with its beauty and uniqueness. He was struck particularly by its captivating lines. He assumed the cost must be at least equal to its look and asked Maurice where he had purchased it. Maurice sheepishly declared that he was the creator of the piece and insisted on its amateurish quality. His humble expressions were politely discounted. He heard only from his friends, "Would you do one for me?"

Maurice thereafter continued with his whittling, enjoying his grandchildren, the ocean, and the sound of the waves.

His creations have been displayed at showings in Vancouver, Canada, Sidney, Australia, San Francisco, and New York.

Of course, as you know, he can't work with his hands.

Nationwide, a belief is held that building principals run the school. Ah, how deeply erroneous and flawed is such thinking. As a school superintendent, I longed for one thing—peace and harmony. I would tell all district principals "Please, don't make waves out there 'cause they splash in my office." They would smile and understand. I truly enjoyed principals who understood.

HAZEL

Occasionally, I encountered a principal who didn't get it. You know the kind—first day of a new school year he holds a four-hour faculty meeting and expounds on all of the exciting things he has been planning all summer. He's full of energy and bubbly—just a ball of lightning and fire. He can make one think bad thoughts, such as can we innocently expose him to several sick children.

The school year had just gotten under way when the young fellow called.

"Hello, Dr. Golarz."

"Yes."

"This Is Jake, Principal of Cleveland Elementary."

"Yes, Jake. I recognize your voice, even at this intense volume."

"Oh, sorry. Is this better?"

"Much."

"Dr. Golarz, we got a problem out here. You know the prep time period—you know, giving teachers a period during the day when they can prep?"

"Go ahead."

"Well, I got a bunch out here who aren't preppin.'"

"What do they look like, Jake?"

"Sir?"

"Are they women, Jake?"

"Yes, Sir."

"Are they older women teachers, Jake?"

106

"Yes, Sir."

"Do they have white hair and are several wearing broaches?"

"That's the bunch."

"Don't go in there, Jake, Do you hear me? DO NOT go in there. That's the varsity in there. Do you understand?"

"But sir, the contract says...."

"Jake, listen. Assume for a moment that the world is a river and that all the people of the world are in canoes. They are all rowing in the river following the current. Jake, find a canoe. Get into the canoe in the river. Row slowly in the direction they are all rowing. If you do not do this, Jake you will make waves that will splash in my office. Do you understand, Jake?"

"I think so, sir."

That late afternoon I got a phone call.

"Dr. Golarz?"

"Yes."

"This is Hazel—Cleveland Elementary."

"Hazel, delighted to hear from you."

"Dr. Golarz, there are four of us who would like to meet with you."

"Hazel, my time is your time. When would you like to meet?"

"If it would not be inconvenient, tomorrow morning before we get to school."

"Certainly, Hazel, at what time?"

"Well, we normally get to school at 6:00 a.m. Would 5:15 be all right?"

"I'm always in my office at 4:45. Look forward to our meeting."

I hung up the phone and sat there for a long moment enjoying uncharitable thoughts about Jake.

The next morning Hazel and the other veteran teachers came in, professionally dressed and not a hair out of place. Hazel began, "Dr Golarz, we arrive at school each morning at 6:00 a.m. This has been our practice for 25 years. We have tea, a light breakfast, and then prepare our classes. We enjoy the solitude. At 7:30 we often assist early arrivals who might need some individualized tutoring. We don't know of this prep time thing that the union gentlemen have worked out with the school board. To us it is of no concern. Now, Dr. Golarz, if you believe that we are doing something wrong, we would like to hear this directly from you, the superintendent."

And now good reader, how would you handle this? Contemplating Jake's under the bus accident?

School superintendents spend a great deal of their time dealing with unpleasant tasks. That's why they visit primary classrooms. Young children are always so enthusiastic and happy. The personnel department is also a place they love to visit, for you will often find teachers new to the profession waiting to see if they can be hired. One late summer day I wandered down to that office hoping to be uplifted.

THIRD GRADE TEACHER

"Dr. Golarz, good to see you here." "Thanks. What are you doing?""Well, we're attempting to hire a third grade teacher and we are down to two finalists. Want to help?" "Love to." "Well, we will send the candidates to you as soon as you complete reviewing their files."

I was really quite excited. The selection of a new teacher is such an awesome responsibility. I opened the first file. I found page after page of outstanding academic work plus a record of many honors and awards. I asked my staff to send in the candidate.

"Young man, would you mind if I asked you a few questions?" "Sure, go ahead." "Why do you want to work here?" "Well, you're not my first choice, but until those other schools districts have an opening I will help you out for a year. I know I'm over qualified for your district, but a year is not too long."

I was stunned—almost speechless. The remainder of the interview went downhill. After he left, I sat for a long moment trying to regroup.

I then opened the second file. I moved from page to page but came up empty. Finally I closed the file and asked staff to send her in. She sat and I said, "Do you mind if I get right to the heart of this?" She replied. "No, not at all." So I said, "You didn't do too well in college, did you?" She smiled, chuckled a bit and said. "That's an understatement." I then said, "I know you must have, at minimum, a GPA of 2.0 or you couldn't have received a diploma." She replied, "Yep, that was my GPA, a solid 2.0."

I then said. "Why do you think we should hire you?" "Well, I know my record looks bad—took me six years to finish. I often had to work two jobs to make it, but I never quit. You see, as an elementary school student I had some great teachers, and I just always wanted to be like them. Also, I love kids, even the tough and mean ones."

Well, we got to talking. Half an hour slipped by. Eventually, almost an hour. I then looked at her and said, "You know, I like you." She smiled and responded, "I like you too. Who are you?" I said, "I'm the superintendent." She laughed and replied, "I like you anyway."

Finally, I said, "I'm going to recommend that we hire you. I have a feeling that you are just what we need."

Later on, In early October, I called Nancy, her principal. "Nancy, can I come over and observe her teach?" "You come over any time. You'll get a kick out of this," and then she said, "We all love her."

The next morning I slipped into the back of her classroom. I was taken aback for she was teaching a relatively sophisticated piece of mathematics. Before I left, I had her join me in the hallway and I said somewhat jokingly, "I didn't think you knew that stuff."

She beamed and sassily replied, "I don't. We're learning it together."

Three years later her colleagues voted her teacher of the year.

I worked in communities of poverty for many years—month after month. Still vivid are memories of rot, decay, of rats, and roaches, of bare unpainted walls, and piles of discarded, soiled clothing and bedding. But of all of these distressing memories it is the look of abandoned dreams, and hopelessness in the faces of the young mothers of those communities that most haunts me.

"THE POOR YOU SHALL
ALWAYS HAVE WITH YOU"

I'll never forget Martha, the young mother who wanted so desperately to share something of pride with me. As she spoke she habitually hid, with her wrist, her mouth for many of her teeth were rotten or gone though she was but 20 years old. She also tried to avoid smiling. She told me of her oldest son, Billy, age six, who could count to five. How proud she was. And all I could think was how very little she understood of the capacities of children that age. She did not tell me of her other four children, nor about her then pregnant condition. She just wanted so desperately to be proud of something.

In late December she delivered. She delivered on an old wooden table in the unheated garage of a neighbor. The delivery did not go well and the full term baby died. Martha lost a great deal of blood giving that birth, and when she returned home that afternoon, her care was in the hands of her young children. The next day, Christmas Eve, she would have died had it not been for a chance and unannounced visit by Mrs. Kucer, a school social worker delivering a food basket. The veteran Mrs. Kucer broke all of the rules that Christmas Eve. With little regard for comfort and or protocol she pulled essential professionals from their hearths and Christmas puddings. Relentlessly, she got Martha life saving care.

Tragically however, she was only able to save Martha's life. My visit to Martha with Mrs. Kucer in subsequent weeks revealed the deeper tragedy. Martha was moving toward the death of her soul. We could both see it. There was no longer the raising of her arm to cover the missing teeth, no smile, no searching for something of pride. Martha was alive but rapidly losing all of the hopes that keep us all alive. As the neighborhood male rapists in sheep's clothing gathered, she simply didn't care anymore. My heart still aches when I recall her face, helpless and broken.

During those years I found it difficult to get empathy from my co workers for the poor I daily worked with, no matter what I said. Finally a very seasoned co-worker, Fred Monberg, said to me, "Take them with you when you visit." I objected, but he insisted. Returning from the first neighborhood visit with four of my co-workers, all was silent in the car. Then one began to weep and exclaimed, "How can they live like that? My God, how?"

I believe that human beings are not evil and insensitive. It's just that many have never seen. I've also found that when directly confronting such atrocities, we, particularly women, are much more empathetic to the observed pain.

Martha, who in life only wanted to be proud of something, died that winter. She died alone on that garage birthing table along with the babe she bore. Tragically, no one saw.

Most tragically, no one seemed to care.

Sunday, October 18, 1936, was game day. The Yellow Jackets semi- pro football team was coming out of the 10:30 a.m. mass at St. Mary's church. The temperature was about 55 degrees and most people walking from their homes and heading to the game had decided to wear a coat of some kind. Chicago Heights brought a fan group numbering about 300. The home crowd numbered nearly 1200. It would be a well-attended contest with a special attendee no one could have predicted.

JEBRONOWSKI'S HORSE

L ate Saturday, Mr. Jebronowski's junk-yard horse had gotten loose, and all day Saturday as well as during the night he had been scavenging in garbage cans up and down the alleyways. By late morning on Sunday, he had decided to pasture and relieve himself between the ten- and- twenty -yard lines on the football field. Players who normally lined the field pregame, found themselves with the added assignment of trying to clean up after a very large horse that must have spent the evening and entire night eating what clearly was not agreeing with his digestive system. Further, they couldn't convince him to move from a location that he had decided was his new home.

The situation did not really get resolved until nearly game time when Mr. Jebronowski was located. He then grabbed the reigns and began leading the horse across the field to the north end while the horse continued defecating. The 40-yard line and the 50 both received a massive load. Each defecation was cheered by the 1500 fans lining the entire length of the field. The last dump, on the opponent's 15 yard line, was preceded by what sounded like a thunderclap from the rear end of the horse and which could be heard from one end of the field to the other. The thunderclap and subsequent load dropped on the 15 was followed by a particularly loud, sustained cheer and men waving their hats. Mr. Jebronowski who somehow mistakenly assumed that the cheering was for him, waved back.

The home team was in a complete state of hysteria. Stretching along the side line near their bench, all were experiencing uncontrolled laughter and those affected most severely had fallen to their knees and were holding their sides. Further, a glance to the other side of the field revealed few Chicago Heights players still able to stand. Finally, the referee took a position in center field and shouted in a voice he hoped would sound authoritative, "Okay, men, we need to play football." This seemed to work for there was a brief period of silence.

Then, simultaneously, as community men rushed onto the field with large shovels and wheelbarrows, Jebronowski's horse, from the end zone, let loose with a final and deafening thunder clap. This visual and auditory occurrence, of men with shovels, wheelbarrows and the deafening sound from the ass of a large horse was like experiencing a perfectly choreographed circus fire drill. The crowd and players tried to establish decorum but it was too late. There were now sustained roars from both sides of the field. The referee simply threw his hands into the air.

Finally the game got underway but no player that afternoon could completely stop his uncontrolled momentary chuckle between plays. There was occasional slipping and sliding by players during the game, but for the most part both teams avoided the center of the field and attempted to play the game near the sidelines.

The game remained a delightful memory for years to come, though no one could tell you the final score.

Whenever I wash and dry my hands, the inside of my right wrist becomes visible to me as does the scar that remains from the deep cut across that wrist. The flashback is immediate as is the memory of my friend Jose.

My Friend Jose, God, and the Rolling Mill

J ose and I met while members of the labor gang in the rolling mill at Inland Steel. We soon developed the habit of having lunch together on the loading dock, he with his tacos and me with my baloney sandwiches.

Most days we worked together. Then one day I was assigned away from the labor gang and Jose. My assignment was at the other end of the rolling mill where we never worked. Specifically, I was assigned to work alone in front of a stack of thin- grade steel sheets that were about four feet square. I was to lift one sheet at a time, hold the sheet up to a light and look for pin holes. Heavy duty gloves and arm guards were essential, for the sheets were thin and sharp. Sheets with pin holes went on a stack to the left and those without pin holes on the stack to the right. After two hours most guys developed a rhythm, after four hours boredom set in, and after six hours, a new stack of steel sheets.

It was about 10 a.m. in the morning. The rhythm portion of the day was ending and I was moving toward boredom. Then I heard an intense loud sound of something like massive steel on steel. The wall of steel sheets in front of me and the steel barrier behind the sheets were being crushed and strewn about like confetti. I remember being struck then all went black.

The next thing I remember was the face of Jose.

"You will be OK. God sent me."

I turned my head and could see blood everywhere. I must have looked frightened for Jose then said.

"Do not be afraid, I stopped the bleeding. God sent me."

I passed out again.

Later that day in the clinic I learned that a large fork lift had backed into piles of steel, pushing those piles into the steel sheets and my work area. The accident resulted in a head injury and a slash across the inside of my right wrist from one of the steel sheets. I had been bleeding a lot but Jose found me and had rigged a tourniquet and stopped the bleeding. Several others had been in the area before Jose but had not seen me.

At lunch on the dock the following week I asked Jose. "Tell me what happened."

He replied. "We did not have enough shovels so they sent me to get more."

"But Jose the shovels are stored on the other side of the plant, nowhere near where I was working."

"I know, but God told me to go find you, so I followed where He told me to go"

It's probable that I would not have been found in time if it were not for Jose. How he found me and why he looked remains understandable only in the spiritual realm. His gift to me was more than my continued temporal life. He reaffirmed my faith.

The Bible tells us that Christ asked Peter to come out and walk on the water. After taking several steps Peter sank. I am quite confident that Jose would have made it to the boat. Such, I believe, was his unwavering faith and what I came to judge was God's reciprocal love for him.

Most teachers and school administrators were ordained before birth to teach. Such was the case of Joe Grayson and his teachers. Their focus was to do everything they could for students.

Help Him to Study the Stars

I was an assistant superintendent when I got Joe's call. "Ray, can you come out to our school and meet with several teachers?"

"Sure, Joe, when?"

"Any chance you can come today?"

"See you after school, Joe."

At 4:30 pm., I met with Joe and five teachers. Joe began. "Ray, we have a young man, age 16 preparing to drop out of school and work at Standard Foundry. We, however, all think he has incredible academic potential. With this in mind, we have created an unorthodox educational experience that we think will keep him in school. Mr. Nelson our physics teacher will explain."

"Dr. Golarz, the boy's name is Richard and his family is quite poor. With money he has saved working at Wleklinski's bowling alley, he is completing the construction of a four-inch reflector telescope in his basement. He ground his own lens and his work is flawless. He would like to add timing mechanisms to follow stars across the night sky, but he currently lacks that skill.

We, his teachers, want to form an interdisciplinary curricular team and assist his growth. His obligation at project's end would be to write a thesis explaining his work and also the completion of the telescope with the functional timing mechanisms. Mrs. Jones, our English teacher, would work with him in the design and preparation of the thesis paper. I would assist him with physics implications, Mr. Jennings would work with the historical aspects of telescopes, Mr.

Thomas with mathematical considerations, and Miss Zerrig with speech, for he will be orally presenting his work. Our obstacle to doing this is that the state requires that we secure a waiver since what we are proposing violates a set of curricular guidelines and regulations."

I then said, "I assume this this is where I come in." They all smiled.

My task was not as difficult as you might imagine At the time, I was working with a school board who were three standard deviations left of center, so they readily agreed to anything that was challenging and adventuresome. In addition, I knew several high ranking state department administrators who made the board appear conservative.

Once the semester began, all seemed to go like clockwork. Then in mid October, there was an unanticipated glitch. A critical part of the timing mechanism would not function half way into an event series. The problem was beyond the capacities of both Mr. Nelson and Mr. Thomas. Therefore, Mr. Thomas with Richard contacted the Planetarium in Chicago. They explained everything and were invited to come to Chicago for a session with two of the planetarium's astronomers.

The rest you can easily surmise. They loved Richard, his enthusiasm, and his work. The teachers that he would interact with now would include two of the planetarium's staff. Each Wednesday he would catch an early morning South Shore train and spend the day in Chicago "studying the stars."

Ultimately, Richard completed his project. His oral presentation was stunning. That Christmas he began his lifelong study, practice, and teaching of astronomy.

When I keynoted conferences and told this story I would often be asked. "Why don't we do this for all children?" My response always was and continues to be, "Give us the necessary funding and resources and we will.

For you see, teachers are ordained before birth. They will do everything they can to help students."

It was a Saturday morning in the summer of 1949. My grandmother (Busia) would go shopping, and I would go with her. The trolley cars were full and clusters of people stood waiting at each stop, hoping to get a place on the way to Chicago.

A Kid's Memorable Summer Day

B usia however, did her shopping locally. My favorite store was the poultry shop. Once inside you couldn't hear yourself think. The sounds of the hundreds of clucking hens, roosters, and chicks filled the air. Feathers were everywhere and filled cages stacked high. The smell filling your nostrils was pure poultry. A long twenty-foot counter separated patrons from the birds. Three or four men were always busily assisting the dozen customers lined up. Busia's negotiating style was extraordinary. She had a timing way about her that brought a second lower-price offer from the clerk before she even stated her initial bid. Then, once he gave that lower price, she had a way of waving him off with her hand and arm that made it clear that he was nowhere near the ball park.

This would go on for several minutes while impatient other customers were, with their body language, putting a pressure on the clerk that Busia was very aware of. Finally, the clerk would throw up his arms and make a plea with a final offer. At that point, if she reached for her change purse, we had a deal. If she began tapping her foot slowly, and looking around at the cages, it wasn't over. Usually, in these cases, the clerk would make a beseeching final stab at resolution. Then Busia would smile, give him a hard nod of her head, pull out the change purse and release the tension of all those behind us. The clerk, though beaten, was glad it was over.

I really loved those Saturday matches.

In the afternoon of that day, my buddy John and I went "ball buzzing" (searching for lost golf balls) on the country club's thirteenth hole. Monday morning was caddy day—free golf for caddies, if you had golf balls.

We hadn't been there more than 15 minutes when a group of golfers from another hole began walking toward our location looking for a lost ball. They weren't really close but John and I decided to hide in the tall grasses. John and I were hiding about 30 feet from one another. Within just a few minutes I observed John shooting straight up from his hiding spot, screaming and then dropping straight back down again. To my amazement he did this incredible athletic feat several times in intervals of about every fifteen or twenty seconds. Finally, in the manner of a pole-vaulter he went straight up, landed on his feet and bolted, as if out of a cannon down the bank and into the river. I could see him from my hiding place running and jumping in zig- zag fashion through the middle of the river while slapping himself everywhere. I had never seen him move so fast or athletically.

When I caught up to him, he was sitting bare assed in the river with his pants pulled down to his ankles. Apparently, he had accidently laid on a hornets' nest that had fallen from a tree. He had bites all over his ass. I tried really hard not to laugh but—you know.

Later, at Busia's house, she gave John some lotion. We then washed, prayed, and I sat down. John sort of did. On the kitchen table we found chicken soup with homemade bread. Finally we lay on the front-room floor and turned on the radio. It would be a great night—The Green Hornet topped off with the Lone Ranger.

It doesn't get better than being ten-years-old in the summertime.

I finished a keynote address in Phoenix when a young teacher came to the stage and handed me a gold colored lapel starfish pin. She said, "Please wear it. You made a difference today." I was taken with this special gesture and asked friends what the starfish pin symbolized. Dr. Dave Hrach, Superintendent of Tombstone, explained, "Ray, it comes from a story written by Loren Eisley. It goes like this."

Mike and the Starfish

One day a man was walking along the beach when he noticed a boy picking something up and gently throwing it into the ocean. Approaching the boy, he asked, "What are you doing?" The youth replied, "Throwing starfish back into the ocean. The surf is up and the tide is going out. If I don't throw them back, they'll die." "Son," the man said, "Don't you realize there are miles and miles of beach and hundreds of starfish? You can't possibly make a difference!" After listening politely, the boy bent down, picked up another starfish, and threw it back into the surf. Then, smiling at the man, he said, "It made a difference for that one."

When I got back home, with the school board's approval we ordered enough pins for all of our staff. A special note went with the starfish pin telling the starfish story and then asking them to wear the pin because they daily made a difference.

The starfish were an immediate hit. Teachers, secretaries, and custodians, seeing each other's pins while in the hardware store or on the street, were giving each other a high five.

Sometime later I was concluding a meeting with principals. As they were leaving, John a high school principal asked if we had any more of the starfish pins. Mike, one of his assistant principals, had given his pin to an aide who had not received one. I advised John that we had ordered more, but at the moment we had none. He seemed disappointed, so I said. "Here, John, take mine, but don't tell Mike where it came from otherwise he might resist taking it." John resisted, but I made him take it.

Several weeks later I got a phone call from John. "Ray, we have an emergency. My assistant principal Mike had a heart attack between classes in a hallway. No one found him lying there until the change of classes. He's being helicoptered to Indianapolis." I hung up and then informed board members. At the hospital Mike was declared to be in critical condition.

The next weeks were stressful, but eventually Mike got home. Soon afterwards we had the high school graduation. Mike's doctors encouraged him not to come. But, really.

In the auditorium, Mike came running up to me and with his forever big smile said. "Dr. Golarz do you know why I'm alive?" I was completely disarmed. He then said, "The starfish." I'm sure I looked puzzled so he continued. "When I lay in the hallway, unable to move, my head was turned to my coat lapel. The sun was shining through the skylight onto my starfish pin and it seemed to be sparkling and glowing at me. That beautiful comforting glow told me that I had something yet to do, and so I hung on." He continued to smile, but I was too choked up to respond. We went on stage and handed out diplomas.

I never told Mike that he wore my starfish pin.

I have come to recognize in my older age that we never really understand the impact of even the smallest gestures of good will. I only know that we should never stop doing so.

Each spring the faculty of Central High would select twenty to twenty-five students from the sophomore and junior classes—students they considered to be the brightest and the best and also manifesting strong leadership potential. Those selected would be invited to attend the summer Student Leadership Conference held near Notre Dame University.

JOHN T. WILLIAMS

One of the students selected the year in question was John P. Williams—honor student, and vice president of the National Honor Society. But his letter of invitation contained a clerical error and the invitation went to John T. Williams. When John T. received the letter he was stunned. He had no idea that he was held in such high esteem.

That summer John T. boarded the conference bus. There was some question as to his being there but he simply provided the invitation letter.

It wasn't until mid fall of the next school year that the error was detected. It was brought immediately to the building principal. He was aghast. How could this possibly have happened? He was told that it was simply a clerical error. He then asked, "Has anyone called from the leadership conference?" He was assured that there had been no call, and students who had attended had not spoken of anything other than their feeling that the experience was productive and worthwhile.

Several weeks later a call came. It came from the president of the board responsible for the leadership conference. The principal took the phone and sat. His thoughts were not positive.

"Are you the principal?" "Yes, I am." "Well sir, we have some extraordinary news for you and would like to share it by phone before the registered letter gets to you. We believed that this personal call would be in order. You see, after the conclusion of each summer conference we the staff and representative students, meet and select one young man and one young woman who we feel exhibited, at the highest level, the kind of leadership our country must have in order to successfully lead and participate in the world of the future. I am so proud to advise you that our selection of the most extraordinary young man for this past summer is your own John T. Williams. He is a rare gift. You should be so proud." Those witnessing the call stated that the principal just sat there for a long moment and then simply said, "Thank you."

John T. did not know a mistake had been made regarding his selection. At the leadership conference he tried to act in a manner that would make those who selected him proud. He wanted to fit in and honor his selection. I know these things for you see John T. was an African American student in my wife's class at that high school— her special education class.

We all noted that John came back to school that fall noticeably sadder. He had attended a summer conference for the "gifted" where they had defined him as someone to be decidedly honored.

That fall upon his return to school, he always entered his special education classroom only at the last moment, just before the bell rang—when the hall was empty of fellow and newly befriended "gifted" students.

John confided in us that his overwhelming fear was that he would be seen by those who had only known him at the summer conference—known him as gifted. If they knew he was special education would they then see him as stupid or handicapped? Might they laugh?

He was quite sure he couldn't handle that.

Could anyone?

Sadly, today most Americans have been convinced that the primary purpose of education is to cause students to become more cognitively proficient in the studies of mathematics, technology and science. Measuring the success or failure of this endeavor is most often assessed by objective testing. Ultimately one's value as a person is defined by a set of these test scores.

AN ISLAND OF CIVILITY

S ome years ago in response to this change that was moving schooling further away from cherished outcomes such as truthfulness, kindness, empathy, and decency, I met with a group of sixty administrators representing elementary, middle and high schools. Could we reverse the trend in our own schools? Could we nudge our school community back to seeing the importance of honorable human qualities? Could we create an island of civility?

We came up with a plan. We would focus the school district on the human qualities we most respected, qualities if instilled in all of us, would change a world needing such change. Our plan was simple. First, we would advise our communities that the development and recognition of such personal qualities was a major purpose of schools. Second, within several months we would ask each school community to identify two teachers, two non-certified staff and seven students from their school who had exhibited in a remarkable way such personal qualities. Finally, at a public school board meeting in the spring, we would recognize and honor all of these persons who had been selected.

Within a short time after implementing the plan, unanticipated changes seemed to occur throughout the district. Many expressed feeling a subtle, quiet peace. Along with that feeling of peace, other significant changes occurred. There were fewer suspensions for fights, the dropout rate went down, and, most notably, a number of teachers who were planning retirement decided to stay.

At a board meeting the following spring, each of those identified received a certificate of honor with their name inscribed and signed by school leaders. The awards were handed to each of them by their own parent or spouse. A reception followed.

I left the district some time after that, but was advised by colleagues that the practice we had initiated continued for the next several years. It was distressing to hear that it ended. I remember being sad at the thought that a very special practice was gone, and I assumed, quite probably, would be forgotten.

Some twenty-five years later, I was scheduled to speak at a conference on Bainbridge Island near Seattle. When I arrived, my host said that a very prosperous business community leader, known for his practices of treating his employees with honor and dignity, asked if he could attend my presentation. I had, of course, no objection. After my presentation we met. I was stunned to learn that he was born and raised in my own home community. He explained excitedly his daily practices of finding ways to dignify his 1,500 employees. He spoke of the culture he was attempting to create and of the awards being given to employees who manifested kindness and generosity.

I was immediately reminded of the practice I had been a part of so many years earlier. I told him about it. He smiled and said, "I know, Dr. Golarz. You see, I was a seventh grader at Lafayette School in those days. My mom was sick and couldn't be at the school board meeting that night, So you handed me my award."

"I shot an arrow into the air, It fell to earth, I knew not where;"
—Longfellow

I was nearing my fifth birthday. My dad, Lefty, and I were in my grandfather's back yard. Dad was searching through the woodpile, for he was doing some carpentry work. I was sitting on the top of the wood pile—a favorite kid's spot.

CHARLIE

" D ad, I have a new friend" "Who, son?"
"Well, you know across the street from our house, past the brick yard and close to the coal yard?" "Yeah."

"Well, there's a black kid there my size. We played last night. His uncle from Chicago came by when we were playin' and asked me who I was. I told him, and he wanted to know if I was Lefty's kid. I said "yes." He said he had played football with you and that you and he had been good friends—told me to tell you that Charlie said "hi." You remember him?"

"Sure do. We grew up together in this neighborhood."

"Tell me about him, Dad."

"He was the fastest kid I have ever known. But, more importantly on a football field he could change directions without losing speed."

"Is that good, Dad?"

"It sure is son. Had he been given the ball more often and also had good blocking, our team would have gone undefeated."

"Did he carry the ball a lot?"

"No."

"Why?"

"Because he was black."

"I don't understand, Dad."

"Ray, just because you're the best, doesn't mean that this world is going to give you what you deserve—especially if you're black. Once in practice, Charlie ran up the middle for a great gain and then lots of players piled on him. When my brother Walt and I got to the pile, we could hear Charlie screaming. We started pulling guys off. When we got to him, we could see that he had huge bite marks all over his legs and arms. We pulled him up and he stood there between Walt and me, shaking."

"What did you do?" "With Charlie between us, we told those guys that if anything like that ever happened again to Charlie, we would come into their neighborhood, find them, and beat the s*** out of them right on the street in the presence of their neighbors and families."

"Did you do it?"

"Didn't have to."

"Why?"

"It never happened again."

"Why?"

"They knew we meant it."

Dad then stopped and just stared for a long moment quietly in the direction of our apartment and the coal yard beyond. Then he said, "Son, climb down from that wood pile. You and an old friend who's visiting some of his family deserve a proper introduction." Later that afternoon Dad introduced me to his friend, Charlie. I said, "Hello," shook hands, and then went off to play with my new buddy in the brick yard. Dad and Charlie sat on the front steps of an old house nearest the coal yard just talking and drinking a couple of beers.

I never saw a black person get physically bitten. But throughout my entire life I have been told of and have seen how systemic racism of black Americans has left agonizing bites on their hearts and their souls.

Why would we ever question their rage?

In the 1960 movie "The Time Machine," George Wells (Rod Taylor) takes three books to a future time to guide the primitive civilization of the "Eloi" to the building of a "brighter" world. The movie does not reveal his choices. Of the millions of books available in the world of today, my first choice would be Stephen Gould's 1981 **"The Mismeasure of Man."**

THE MISMEASURE OF MAN

I t is abundantly clear that most of us do not see one another as equals. The flaw in such backward thinking is causal to holding back not only the potential of every human being but also the evolution of a worldwide middle class. Gould's analysis of this discrimination issue is masterful. He gives no quarter to arguments supporting and calling for racial inequality. He systematically demonstrates with scientific evidence the clear argument for egalitarianism. There is no biological evidence to support inequality. Unequal educational opportunities, unequal job opportunities and unequal housing opportunities are man-made differences; God had nothing to do with such.

Aggressive challenges must take place. If we don't do so, there will be many who will fall victim to believing the myths of inequality and will see nothing wrong with perpetuating the tragic and inhumane behaviors that are rampant today.

Not long ago, when I disembarked from an American Airlines flight to the Deep South where I was to keynote a conference, I kept saying to myself, "Ray, stop presuming that systemic racism still exists here." The superintendent who picked me up insisted that we drive past his bus garage before going to the hotel. I was tired but he insisted. At his bus garage we drove back and forth, row after row. Finally, I said, "Jim, I didn't realize that your school district was so large." He turned to me and said, "It isn't Ray. We don't bus the blacks with the whites."

We all sit in the evenings in our living rooms naively thinking that the passage of civil rights legislations and court decisions like *Brown v. Board of Education* have finally made permanent differences. Tragically, there continues to be generations of adults who exhale with each breath their hatred of equality upon their posterity. Their children then inhale this detestation. They become the white supremacists of today and tomorrow. For them, laws enacted to fight discrimination carry no weight.

Years ago a teacher friend and I drove to Tampa, Florida. Nearing Florida we noticed that we needed gas. We had foolishly passed gas stations easily accessible from the expressway. We, therefore, left the expressway and found a small town with a station. As we pumped the gas, we could not help notice that we were being slowly surrounded by seven or eight local men, some holding tools such as lug wrenches. When we filled the tank, an apparent leader emerged and said to us, "You haven't paid the town tax. That will be $40.00." They were all now quite close to us. Without arguing, we pulled from our wallets the amount demanded. When we got into our car, the apparent leader leaned into our open car window and said with a smile, "You N***** lovers best not ever stop here again. Got it?" I have never understood hate, but know it when I see it. I am convinced that if either of us had been black, we and our car would never have been found. Clearly systemic racism in *our* primitive culture has never ended.

So I ask, as did George's friend Filby at the end of *The Time Machine*.

Which book would you choose to assist the Eloy in the creation of a new and brighter future?

In 1946 Dad bought a 1937 Buick Opera Coupe. It was built like a truck. The gauge of the steel approximated the American tank. He kept it in the garage that he and his father had built.

But Water Runs Through It

When he was not at work and his car was not in his garage, he would perform any number of operations on it: oil changes, carburetor adjustments, spark plug changes, brake adjustments, wheel alignments, replacing kingpins and brake linings. These sessions were always capped off with washings, simonize treatments and a bottle or two of Schlitz beer. He loved that car.

The only real defect of the car was its extensive underbelly rusting and subsequent holes in various places of the floor from salty winter roads. In winter the cold air coming up from the icy streets made the car's heater useless. This didn't bother dad though. He was one of the old warrior breed. Mom always brought a blanket to cover her and younger siblings. Dad just grinned, sang a little *Al Jolson*, and drove on.

The back seat of the car was made up of two small opera seats. They each had a steel rod at their base that was intended to rest on a small metal plate on the floor and thus be level and function as viable seats. The plates had long ago busted through, so my brother Joe and I had to sit in the back seat area angled toward the floor. We would look down and watch through the floor holes as the streets zipped by beneath our feet. Rain water would spray up into the back seat if Dad drove too close to the curb where rain run-offs accumulated. We learned quickly not to sit behind the driver's seat, for that's where the tsunami always hit. We fought for the passenger side rear seat.

Our short struggle would usually result in our squeezing together, starboard side.

One time Dad, Joe, and I, ages seven and nine, were finishing a pre-Christmas visit at Dad's parents' home. Dad promised to take an older kid home who had also been visiting. We knew the kid because he had bullied Joe any number of times. He had an ugly disposition. When we came out of the house he shoved Joe to the ground on his way into the rear seat behind Dad's driver seat. He then exclaimed, "I'm sitting here, punks." Joe tried to caution the kid but he said, "Shut up, punk." I motioned to Joe to come over and sit with me and then said, "Joe, he's our guest." Joe objected, "But, Ray…" I said again, "guest, Joe, guest."

Dad then raced into the car through a falling, icy heavy rain, slammed his car door, and exclaimed, "Hang on, guys." He hung a left at the corner and headed south. The winter rain was falling, but Dad was in a hurry.

The rest happened quickly. He gunned it then made a sharp cut into the outside lane near the curb. Immediately the rush of icy water overwhelmed the windshield and entire car. From the other side of the back seat, Joe and I heard this bloodcurdling, intense scream. We looked in the direction of where the kid had been sitting, but it was like trying to find him in the middle of Niagara Falls. Eventually, as the icy water dripped down, his face reappeared.

Joe and I tried not to laugh but it was hard—really hard.

It was a beautiful fall day and I was preparing to leave my office for the weekend. Five minutes before the switchboard closed a call came in.

"Ray?" "Yes." "This is Phil—Central High."

I had determined over the years that calls from assistant principals needed to be a priority. "Phil, what can I do for you?"

OFF THE RECORD

"Ray, I have enrolled thousands of kids over the years, but rarely have I enrolled a kid that frightened me as much as the one I just enrolled. Nice looking kid, kind of preppy and well dressed--came in with his aunt. Papers all in order—transfer from some academy in California. Ray, just looking into this kid's eyes scared the hell out of me and gave me cold chills. A lifetime of working with kids tells me something is wrong. I tried to get someone by phone from this academy, but no luck."

I asked Phil what I could do and he replied. "You're an assistant superintendent. Possibly someone will respond to you." I advised him that I would try. My first several calls resulted in dead ends. Finally, I decided to attempt a different approach. I asked for the psychologist. I hit the jackpot.

"This is Dr. Wilson, how can I help you?"

I explained the urgency of my call. After a long silence he replied. "I'm sorry I can't help you."

I persisted and again explained the importance of my call. Finally, he said,

"Off the record?"

I responded, "I'll take it any way I can get it." He then began, "Off the record. About a month ago he attempted to rape an aide in one of our housing units. Five days ago he was caught in the act of attempting to rape a night nurse. The next day we were facing a staff walkout. He has been properly cleared to leave the institution, so he is legally yours. Remember, this is off the record." He then hung up.

I knew the law as well as Supreme Court decisions. The kid had a property right to an education. But what if he rapes a girl in our school? How do I explain this to a parent? How does Phil?

I called Phil. I explained everything I had come to know. I then advised him that I was directing him not to enroll this boy. I told him that I was putting this in writing and would deliver this directive tonight to him at his home. There was a long silence and then Phil replied. "Ray, you don't need to bring the letter. Having heard all that you just shared, I wasn't going to let him in anyway." We both laughed, as comrades do. I told him to call me Sunday and we would strategize, but not to call during the Bears-Packers game. We laughed again.

On Sunday at halftime Phil called.

"Ray, you sitting?" "Yes."

"Last night at 1:30 a.m., our young fellow was arrested by Jimmy and Ted from narcotics for attempting to sell marijuana and cocaine. I told Jimmy I would let you know."

"Thanks Phil, but how did Jimmy and Ted know to keep an eye on him?" There was a long pause then Phil replied. "Let's just call it good police work and leave it at that." I paused and then replied. "Thanks Phil, thanks a lot." "Never mind Ray, let's just get back to the game." I hung up, glanced at my two daughters playing safely in our back yard, then went back to the game in the living room with my sons. The halftime was concluding. Bears were up by 13.

There are countless administrators and teachers throughout this nation who are daily faced with these same kinds of moral decisions. Though circumstances for them may be different, they choose to risk on the side of the common good, reasonableness, and the safety of their students. They do not hesitate.

*In the movie **The Grapes of Wrath,** the Joad family finds a camp of civility. Henry Fonda states to the camp custodian, "Ma's gonna like this place, she ain't been treated decent for a long time."*

The following essay was written with the assistance, experience, and insight of Dan Golarz, a Math teacher with experiences on Native American Reservations, LA Schools, China, and South Korea and also Dr. Jessica Balsamo, Student Teacher Supervisor, Concordia University, Madison, Wisconsin. The insights that they provided in several extensive phone conversations provided the substance of these following passages.

Why They Leave

After driving hours, the first year teacher is directed to the personnel office. She's not eaten nor yet found a place to stay the night. She is unsure of herself—nervous. Once in the personnel office, she is told to sit and wait. Eventually, she is called up and asked for the completed forms. "What Forms?" "The ones at the end of the counter in the box marked new staff. You're new, right? Fill them out. Don't forget to attach your fingerprinting information." At 5:30 she leaves. She finds the $45 dollar parking ticket beneath her car window wiper—"reserved for administrators only."

Reporting day: "These are your keys, don't lose them. If you do, we must replace the lock. Cost to you will be $150.00. Use only the bathroom on your floor. If you need to copy more than 50 pages per week you will need to purchase your own paper. The manual being provided to you has all the information regarding our computerized systems of grading, keeping attendance, and all the policies and regulations teachers must be aware of. You do not have your own classroom. Your class assignments will require that you move from room to room. Some classroom assignments will not be near one another. Don't erase any chalk boards. What you find on the chalkboard belongs to the teacher who has that assigned room. If a classroom doesn't have sufficient chairs, look for a custodian."

Day one: First, she has three periods of Basic English, 30 to 35 in each class primarily made up of freshman with some sophomores who had failed. Period two in the basement had only 20 chairs. Half hour lunch, then three more teaching periods—two basics and one regular English. Period seven is the prep period. In periods two, three, four, and five students were almost totally out of control. She had never been taught meaningful classroom management. Further the buzzer to call for help was useless. Only once did someone come—25 minutes after her request for assistance. There were no books for three classes. The veteran teacher next door in third period was a lifesaver. Stayed until 6:30, then went to car, shook uncontrollably then cried.

A camp of civility Janesville, Wisconsin while under the leadership of Superintendent Dr. Tom Evert was one of the true camps of exemplary civility. Mike McKinnon provided the structure. For four days prior to the reporting of veteran staff, new teachers were brought on board, given time to interact with one another, shown affordable community rentals, introduced to and given extensive time with their assigned veteran full year mentor teacher located in their building, and had work sessions, always followed by refreshments that introduced them to all of the computerized systems.

Dr. Evert always explained. Teachers do the teaching. They do it uniquely, classroom by classroom. The give and take in each classroom is at the heart of learning. The school board, the central office, and building leadership exist to support. Though the community has the obligation to decide "what "is taught, it is each teacher's authority to judge and carry out "how" that teaching will look. There will be no block scheduling, no grading of teachers based upon student performance.

There will be no reaching for the steering wheel from the back seat.

The name that we affectionately used for her was "Busia," the word for grandmother. On her property was a magnificent apple tree planted at the height of the great depression in 1935. Each summer it would bear wonderful fruit. Pies, canned apples, and apple butter came from that fruit tree.

TREASURE THE ELDERS

I can remember seeing her angry only once. It happened on a warm, mid-summer day on the side of the house where that apple tree grew. My brother Joe and I had gotten into an apple-throwing war with neighborhood kids. The warring weaponry was apples that had fallen to the ground. When Busia saw us, she rushed into the yard. She was livid. It was an anger that neither of us had ever seen before. The warring enemy ran and we were alone with her.

As she pointed her finger at us, shaking it repeatedly, we could see that her anger had brought her to tears. Our immediate assumption was that we had provoked her wrath as a consequence of fighting. We were wrong. Through her broken English we began to understand something very different. We, her grandsons, had been abusing a gift of precious food that God in his goodness had given to her and her family. She was ashamed and disgraced. Still sobbing, she picked up the battered apples lying on the ground, brushed off the dirt and, gently placed them into her apron. She left us there feeling a shame we had never before felt.

Every year I had watched her faithfully plant and tend her garden and her fruit trees. I had even assisted her with the plants, pulling the weeds and hoeing the soil. But until we had seen her express such anger, neither I, nor my brother Joe, had understood what this all meant to her. This growing, nurturing, and eventual harvesting was not just a way of life—it was a daily communion with her God. Each plant and each tree was an act of faith that would bring a response in the form of a harvest—a response promised to an old peasant woman who understood and cherished this bond.

The next spring as my brother and I helped her plant her garden, we saw her do things that we had never before noticed. She spoke quietly to the seeds and the new sprouts. She tended to the soil around them ever so gently, noticing where additional soil might be needed or pressed more firmly. As weeks went by and we moved with her along the rows of plants, we could see that she knew each one, even anticipating what their needs might be. We were seeing things that we had not been previously aware of.

In the late summer and fall, the harvesting of her trees and plants was done in the manner of one accepting gifts from someone of whom you are very fond. During those times, she often hummed the tunes I believe she carried to this land from her home in the old country. They were probably tunes she had hummed as a child assisting with the harvestings or as she walked through meadows tending the animals.

I have not, since my experiences with Busia, spent my life with farmers. As I grow older, I wish I had. I'm not sure that any of us should ever get too far from the soil, or from the elders who can teach us so much. Somehow they seem to have learned better how to spend their lives in simple harmony with their God.

I was moving to a new superintendency. Colleagues advised against it. They warned that teacher union leadership there was hostile. Against all advice, I accepted the offer to go.

An Honorable Union Leader

When I arrived, threats of strike were in the air. Eventually, a one-year contract was agreed to, just in time to move to a new round of negotiations. Those years were brutal. I was confidentially advised that the hostility we were experiencing could be traced directly to the former superintendent's public statement: "Union leaders are not very bright. If they had been, they would have known that I had a full additional percentage to bargain with. They settled for less than what they might have secured."

I asked administrators to adopt the demeanor of peaceful non-aggression. Despite this, hostility continued for two years. It seemed that it was time to plead for a halt. Therefore, during a very tense teacher/administrator meeting I blurted out, "I don't know who you were married to before but I'm not that person." The room grew silent.

Then Stu, the long time leader of the teachers association, pulled from his wallet an old, faded and warn pay stub of $12.75 that he had received after the strike many years ago. He had kept it in his wallet to remind him to never trust administrators. He slowly tore up the pay stub and said, "It's time." Things changed almost immediately. My associate, Dr. Broadwell and I were invited to a "teachers only" bar for a beer. Stu sent word to me that he wanted to consider cooperative bargaining. We selected a highly-regarded Bloomington, Indiana attorney, Bob Cambridge, to facilitate the process.

An appropriate setting was essential, so we rented a retreat center on the Earlham College campus. Each session included catered breakfasts and lunches. Participating teachers were given time off and substitutes were hired for their classrooms. Our goal was to create contract language that would enhance the dignity and self respect of teachers. Existing boiler plate language would be eliminated. The bargaining was done by teachers, administrators and board members. In late mornings and early afternoons, clusters of participants could be seen gathered in grassy areas among the large trees, working on various contract language sections.

One such section Bereavement read as follows: "Teachers are permitted five days of absence for the death of a parent, spouse, child or grandparent and two days for a close relative, close to be determined by the personnel director. Deaths of any others will not warrant paid days." That language was changed to: "When a loved one dies, and you alone decide who a loved one is, take the time you need."

When bargaining concluded there was a sense of peace. Everyone knew that something special had occurred. That last day I stood by a pasture fence with Stu. We watched some horses graze. We didn't speak—didn't have to.

Years later I was keynoting a conference in Atlanta. In the first row were teachers and administrators from that school district. I asked, "What are you doing here?" "We came to hear you. Would you tell them the story of our bereavement language? Since its adoption, no one has ever taken more than five days." I replied, "But they could." "No, Dr. Golarz, we will never give a new superintendent or school board a reason to destroy what we fashioned with our hearts."

At Stu's funeral his mother gave me a copy of his obituary. She said, "He wanted you to have it. He wanted you to note that it says he led teachers in the first cooperative bargaining process. It always made him so proud."

In my youth I worked in steel production plants, usually as a member of a labor gang. When we lacked a full complement of laborers, we worked in a gang of two or three, rather than the normal five. Those were the most difficult of days, for the task of shoveling tons of manganese or other steel ingredients did not diminish because of fewer workers.

LIFT THAT BALE

O n those days, even though the temperature in the plant would reach 120 degrees by noon, even though we would weaken from the continuous heat of the open hearth furnaces, even though water was often unavailable, we would work at a feverish pace. By early afternoon the cramping would begin. Then, despite the rescue of water and salt, our bodies would sometimes give way and the more intense pain would take us to the ground screaming in agony.

At the end of the shift, we would drop our shovels and just sit and stare silently into empty space. Eventually, we would move, not with the quick step of winners, but rather with the shuffling steps of the shackled. We had finished the day, and the piles of steel making ingredients were no more. They would be replaced for our next shift, but for the moment they were gone. There was now an empty space where the ingredients had been.

Throughout my years as a school superintendent, I often saw this besieged look on the faces of teachers and building administrators as I walked the halls of their schools at day's end. I stopped momentarily in their open doorways and, often without their knowing, observed them as they sat and silently stared exhausted into empty space. During earlier parts of those same days, I saw them in their rooms and offices working harder and faster to complete the ever-evasive task. I observed as they skipped their lunch breaks.

Did they shovel, heavily perspire, and cramp? No, but in a way, their work was harder. You see, when the job is to shovel, you can, at day's end, see that the piles of steel ingredients are gone. New piles will replace these, but for the moment you can see that you made a difference. This understanding that you accomplished something, like nothing else, affirms your effort and gives you the strength to return.

In the role of teacher or school administrator there is no smaller pile as the end of the day nears. Despite your best efforts, at day's end the pile is often bigger. You're unsure that you made any progress at all. All you know for sure is that you are exhausted.

Several years ago, I keynoted the administrative retreat of one of the largest school districts in Texas. At dinner the night before, I asked the superintendent's permission to begin my presentation with this statement: "As hard as you try, the task that you and your teachers have been asked to perform cannot be completed." He agreed. So, I began my keynote address with those words. For the next full three minutes, neither I nor the conference coordinators could stop the spontaneous standing ovation. The statement had struck a raw nerve.

Once in a while, teachers and building administrators just need to hear the truth screamed out loud. Does it mean that tomorrow they will walk into work and refuse to pick up their shovels? No, not at all. If anything, they will probably shovel with more intensity. Why? Because, finally someone has affirmed and recognized the truth. The job can't be completed. With that affirmation, they can work with pride.

They can work with pride and honor—not with doubt, guilt, or shame.

The focus of this short story is a midsummer adventurous day in the lives of four pre-teen second generation Polish American boys. The year is 1951. The setting is a Polish neighborhood near Chicago. The plan of the boys for the day is to go river rafting. However, in the early morning of this planned day of exploration the boys could hardly know that in the late afternoon they would experience ethnic hatred directed at them. You, the reader, will watch this experience and see how so many American children are scarred and what the initial open wound does to their feeling of self and self worth. On your journey through this story you will meet the brothers Ray and Joe ages 11 and 9. You will also meet gregarious Bobby and laid-back Stefan, both age 12. The final personality you will get to know is "Busia" the immigrant grandmother. She speaks broken English mixed with Polish. So, when she speaks it is not that we have misspelled words or missed parts of words. Rather we have attempted to capture her speech phonetically. Join them now in the pre breakfast moments of that summer day.

"Zippity Doo Dah"

"Where we goin' Ray?" "I told ya, Joe, on a raft in a river. But stop talkin' about it or Busia will be askin' a lot of questions."

"O.K., Ray."

"Rajmund, you beh get egg from coop."

"O.K., Busia. I'm goin.'"

I ran out to the chicken coop and got six eggs for our breakfast.

As we finished eating, there was knocking on the back side door. Busia, from the back porch exclaimed, "Rajmund, Bobby eh Stefan beh here." Then she said to the visitors, "You beh come in."

Bobby said to Busia, "Thanks, Busia. Want a fresh doughnut from the O.K. Bakery?"

Busia beamed. Bobby knew that an O.K. Bakery doughnut was her soft-spot.

I gave Bobby a dirty look.

"What? What!!"

"You know what."

Then Bobby asked, "Rajmund, you got an empty bag?"

I found a bag and shoved it in his chest while Busia poured her hot coffee to drink with what she didn't understand was her stolen doughnut. Bobby then said to Joe, "Hey, kid, you comin' with us?"

Joe, finishing up his eggs, just smiled and nodded. Then Stefan reminded Joe, "Don't forget the new slingshot we made for you."

Joe pointed to his left rear pocket. Then Busia questioned, "Where you going?"

"Just bummin' around, Busia. Don't worry."

Five minutes later we were out the back side door, the four of us, each with slingshots hangin' out of our back pockets and Bobby with a fairly sizable bag of booty.

"O.K., Bobby, so what did you get?"

"Ten, Rajmund, ten, a new record. Well, now nine, figuring the one I gave to Busia."

I interjected, "I told you before, you can't give Busia stolen shit."

"O.K. O.K. Next time I'll pay for hers. Still feel sticky—had 'em all under my shirt. Looked like Stefan when I came out of the bakery."

Stefan objected angrily, "I ain't fat, Bobby. I'm big-boned. My Ma told me so."

"Well, then, you got the bones of a rhino."

"Gonna kick your ass right here, Bobby."

I jumped in and separated them and then said, "C'mon, guys. C'mon. It's a bright sunny day and we're on our way to have fun on the river. So, let's not ruin it with another fight."

Soon we had left the familiarity of the neighborhood and began the one mile walk to the Little Calumet river. Bobby eventually parted with four of the doughnuts, including the one for himself. So, the talk and camaraderie became pleasant and would have remained so all the way to the river had Bobby not told Stefan that the doughnut he gave to him came from under Bobby's armpit. Nonetheless, we made it and stood just east of Calumet Avenue on the bank of the river.

There wasn't much around that area—a few stores and a gas station, but virtually no homes. Further south Calumet Avenue eventually got to Ridge Road, the ancient shore of Lake Michigan. But we weren't going that way. Today was a river trip. A couple of months earlier Bobby and I had found an old raft that probably had drifted this way from somewhere near Chicago. It was kind of beat up. So, we had made several trips with leftover tar from East Hammond backyard sheds. The last time here, we had tested the raft and we found it to be reasonably seaworthy. With us on this trip, besides

Bobby's stolen doughnuts, we had six potatoes and matches. If we could get a good fire goin' later, the potatoes would only take about an hour. Nothin' like a hot potato out of a fire on a stick. Nothin' like it. Kid brother Joe seemed really excited. This was his first venture out with the guys. Bobby liked Joe a lot. So, Joe bein' three years younger was never a problem.

"Hey, Ray, Bobby, is this it?" Joe had found the raft.

"Good going, Joe."

"Stefan, help Joe get that brush off the raft and let's get under way."

Within ten minutes we were ready to head to the center of the river. We were a little apprehensive cause we had never done it with four guys. In addition, the last couple of weeks there had been a lot of rain, so the river was much deeper than normal. Even with the heavier load the raft was holding up well, but despite its seaworthy nature and our confidence, we had decided to roll up our pants legs. We had two long, sturdy poles that Bobby and I had made a month earlier and with them we pushed off. Once in the river, it didn't take us long to figure out that this raft ride was gonna be a one-way trip. The river current wasn't treacherous, but it was unquestionably strong. The two poles we had wouldn't be enough to go back up stream. Wherever we decided to leave the raft, we'd have to come back for it another day when the river current was not so strong.

"Rajmund."

"Yeah, Bobby."

"Big bend comin' in the river and if you haven't noticed, we're goin' faster."

"Everybody hang on."

Up ahead the river appeared to have rapids, and it must have been making a sharp turn because in the distance it looked like it dead-ended and just disappeared. Then we got to the bend and the rapids. But the momentum had us going right toward some big rocks and not turning with the river. Then we hit. Joe got loose from my arm and Bobby grabbed him. Stefan's pole cracked like a twig and he nearly got pitched overboard. Then the raft turned and began to head more slowly downstream. It had happened so quickly that we hadn't had time to get scared.

I looked down at Joe under Bobby's arm, then at Bobby. All of a sudden Stefan jumped up and screamed, "The doughnuts!" A moment later we all started laughing—then roaring. Maybe we were finally just scared, and somehow Stefan's scream about the remaining doughnuts just had us all cut loose. We had just shot our first rapids on a great river. We still had one pole, a bag of potatoes, and we were alive. Nothin' gets better than that when you're ten. Nothing. Soon, we started to sing. Joe started us off. It was from a movie we all knew, and the moment couldn't have been more appropriate to the song, *"Zippity doo dah, zippity aye, my oh my, what a wonderful day, plenty of sunshine comin' my way. Zippity doo dah, zippity aye."*

We just sang, and sang, and sang all the way down that river. All the way till the river forked.

"All right, guys. This is our stop."

"Rajmund's right, Bobby chimed in. Get ready to jump."

Stefan added, "I'll try to push us to the shore with the pole."

What happened next wasn't quite great seamanship, but we all managed to jump and not get totally soaked. We were now on land and moving south alongside of this large tributary that fed into the Little Calumet. We all noticed that its current was actually swifter than the larger river we had just left.

Stefan shouted out, "Rajmund, where we headed?"

"To the dam up ahead. Bobby and I were here 'bout a month ago."

Then Bobby interjected, "Let's find a place to cook the potatoes somewhere around here in these deep woods so they'll be ready for us on the way back."

"Good idea."

Bobby took the lead. Then he looked back for us and as he did, he tripped over one of the many half-buried fallen trees and fell flat on his face in the mud and leaves. As we rushed to see if he was hurt and gathered around him, he looked up, spit out some leaves, got to his knees and shouted a Polish curse, "Pshaw-clef, oletta."

Joe's eyes got very wide and big. Then Bobby looked directly at Joe and said, "Don't ever say that. It's not very nice." Joe smiled.

Stefan added, "You been hangin' around your dziadzia (grandfather) too much, Bobby."

We finally got to a good spot. Then we dug a hole nice and deep, filled it with some dry bigger, slow-burning logs, then added our six potatoes right in the middle. We covered the whole thing with some kindling and some smaller logs and then cleared away all the dry brush from around the area. Within ten minutes we had a roaring fire. We waited about ten more minutes for the fire to calm down. Then when it did, we threw on some more twigs and several big logs for good measure. We all felt that we had done a pretty good job. So, now we were on our way back to the river and the dam. We figured the dam to be about a half-mile walk, at most, and before we got there, we would be able to hear the water coming over the dam.

It didn't seem to take any time at all for the woods to thin of the massive trees and simultaneously for more and more light to come rushing through from above to touch larger and larger patches of the ground as well as lower branches of the younger trees. We were leaving the forest. The distant light was even brighter than the light now around us and the faint sound that initially defied identification was now clearly the sound of rushing water. And then there it was. There is hardly a memory so deep and pure as the memory of coming through a pristine forest, though small it might be, on a summer afternoon with friends, also age 10, whose senses, like yours, are virgin to the experience that awaits. I don't remember stopping, though we must have. I just remember Joe saying, "Wow!" Bobby and I looked down at him standing between us, then recognized that we were all motionless, just standing in awe. For us, it might as well have been the Niagara Falls, and it was now ours. We had travelled the mighty river, trekked through the primeval forest and together had found the great waterfall.

A primitive, collective yell went up from all of us as we ripped off all of our cloths. Within minutes we were splashing in the waters wearing nothing more than what God had given us as we entered this earth at the moments of our births. We splashed, dove in and out, cannon-balled where we could, horse-played, splashed some more, held our breath under water, and eventually sat together on the shore, or just lay there and soaked up the good sun. No one spoke. Time just drifted by as we simply lay there and enjoyed the moment. A good twenty minutes or so went by then Joe exclaimed. "Hey, Bobby!"

"Yeah, Joe."

"Look at these little round rocks around the edge of the water. They're like marbles."

Bobby excitedly exclaimed, "Rajmund, Stefan, look. Little Joe's right. They're absolutely perfect for ammunition for our sling shots and there's hundreds of em', maybe thousands."

We were dressed within a flash—then carefully collected and loaded our pockets. It's not often you find a perfect rock for your slingshot and here Joe had found hundreds of them. As we sifted through the sand, it was almost impossible to find bad ones, except maybe a few that were too big. All the way back to our potatoes in the deeper woods we fired randomly. We fired at tree trunks in the distance. We fired at leaves, branches, and occasionally birds, though with all the noise we were making, the birds seemed to know to keep their distance.

Finally, we arrived at our fire and the potatoes. Our timing couldn't have been better. Bobby, Stefan, and I sharpened some sticks with our knives. We then uncovered the potatoes. As we pierced their skins with our sticks, it was clear that they were ready and so were we. We took all of them out and then waited a bit for them to cool enough to bite into.

"Hey, Bobby."

"Yeah, Rajmund."

"Stefan says you have a birthday comin' up."

"Yeah…be twelve in about a week."

"Twelve? Bullshit. You're gonna be eleven, like me."

"Gonna be twelve. Got held back in first grade. Stefan's already twelve. Got held back too. You're the only smart one, Rajmund."

I didn't say anything. Just sat there eating my potato. Never knew that about Bobby and Stefan. Some things you just never get told about, I guess.

The potatoes were about the best we had ever eaten, probably because we were so hungry. Then we walked back to that place near the Calumet River where we had left our shoes. On the way we shot at every tree, every telephone pole. We even shot at some carp in the river. Didn't get any though. Once we got back to Calumet Avenue and began heading back to our neighborhood, Joe started singing "Zippity Doo Dah" again, so we all joined in. It was great. We sang for several blocks, even making up words when we couldn't remember some. We were havin' a ball.

Then, right about the time we got to 169th Street, Bobby stopped in front of this little corner grocery store. "Guys, we're gonna have a treat. See, I been holdin' out on ya'." Then he reached into his right front pocket past all of the remaining little rocks and pulled out a dime. He then held it up for us to see.

"Little Joe, how many Hostess cupcakes in a package?"

Joe quickly responded, "two."

"And how much for a package of cupcakes, Joe?"

"A nickel."

"Right again. And I have a dime. So we can buy how many, Joe?"

Joe hesitated, but Stefan and I shouted out, "four."

Then Bobby responded, "Treat time—let's go."

The three of us followed Bobby into the store where there were already several adult customers and a clerk who was up front behind the counter. No sooner had we entered the store than the clerk, a fairly big, husky man, shouted to us, "You little kids, get the hell outta here."

Bobby responded, "but we're here to buy some cupcakes."

"You didn't hear what I said?"

"Why you bein' so mean, mister?"

"You little shits live down there?" as he pointed north toward East Hammond.

"Yeah," replied Bobby.

Then he came very quickly out from behind his counter with a long axe handle, and as he came toward us he yelled, "Get your Polish asses outta here. I don't want you little Polack sons-of-bitches in here, and I don't have to sell to you."

We were all backing out as quickly as we could for he had the long axe handle raised over his head. Bobby was peddling backwards and tripped over Stefan and then went down in the doorway. The little rocks from his pockets went everywhere and his slingshot fell at his feet. By this time the man had reached Bobby and, seeing the slingshot, smashed it with the end of his axe handle while I grabbed Bobby under his arms and pulled him onto the sidewalk outside of the store. The man then stood in the doorway and yelled, "Now, get your little Polack asses back to your own neighborhood before I call the police."

As we ran, we yelled some vulgarities and profanities, but we knew even as we did that it did no good. Within a few minutes, we got to Columbia Avenue, turned left and kept running all the way to the city incinerator and massive water tower. We were back in the neighborhood. We hadn't said much on the way. We had been running most of the way. When we got to Stefan's house, he went his way and from his doorstep simply turned and waved goodbye. Next was Bobby's on Kenwood Street. When we got there, now walking, Joe grabbed Bobby's sleeve and tugged on it several times. Bobby looked down and Joe said, "Our Busia has lots of kapusta, so you have to come to our house and eat with us."

Bobby looked down at Joe and gave him a kind of affectionate laugh and so did I. Then I said, "Tell your Ma you gotta stay with us tonight."

Bobby looked at me then down again at Joe who was smiling. He nodded and went and told his Ma.

When we walked into Busia's back side door, she came out from the kitchen, looked down at the three of us, chuckled with her belly shaking, and as she smiled she shook her head, "Yeh beh clean first, then yeh eat, but you not eat till you beh clean, and don't make mess in bathroom."

Three forest and river warriors hit the tub all at once and after some vicious scrubbing and drying, we were sitting at a kitchen table much hungrier than we thought we were. Busia's bright smile and warm kapusta and buttered rye bread were pushing back an ugly experience and unanticipated pain. Bobby and I, though we did not speak of it that day, were most upset with ourselves not seeing it coming.

Such ugliness directed at us had not been our first time, nor did we expect it to be our last. Like our parents before us, we had grown up in the safety of our Polish neighborhood where we were known and could, therefore, completely relax in our personal uniqueness and community ethnicity. We had also over the years come to understand that this kind of safety and security ended at the neighborhood boundaries.

Two things for sure would come out of this day. No matter what, we would not again be caught off guard. It would again happen—this vile unprovoked ugliness, but we would see it coming. The next time and the time after, we would remain forever vigilant. We would be ready. Secondly and more importantly, no matter what, we would never deny our ethnicity or kowtow to any power or authority in order to get ahead. We would, through harder and sustained work, achieve that for which we strived. Then, if denied, it would have to be for something other than our performance. Like our parents and grandparents before us, we would remain strong and proud.

That night after supper, Busia let us lie on the floor in the living room and listen to some of our favorite radio programs. On this particular night first was "Captain Midnight." Then a real treat in the form of "The Lone Ranger." And finally "Straight Arrow." Halfway through "Straight Arrow" Joe fell asleep. Aunt Rose gave us her bed in the front bedroom that night. She sometimes did that when it was two or three of us and, therefore, a bit too tight for the single bed in the middle bedroom. Bobby and I put Joe in the middle so there'd be no worry about his falling out or being kicked out during the night.

As we all lay there starting to doze off, Joe half asleep said, "Ray, was that real mad guy in the store talkin' about me too?"

Before I had a chance to respond, Bobby said, "No, little Joe, he wasn't talkin' about you. He was just talkin' about us big guys. Right, Rajmund?"

"Right, Bobby."

Then Bobby quietly said to Joe.

"Now you just go to sleep and don't worry about that stuff, Joe."

Joe quietly responded, "Okay."

After a while, I looked over at Bobby and in the dim moonlight saw a tear slowly work its way down the side of his nose. He glanced up at me, saw me looking at him then brushed it aside and said, "Got somethin' in my eye." He then turned over. Shortly thereafter I did too.

Joe and I had an older brother who died before we ever got to know him. As I drifted off to sleep that night, I remember thinkin' that Bobby would have been a good older brother.

During the great depression of the 1930s people, in winter, would walk railroad tracks with gunny sacks. They would search for coal that had fallen from coal trains. Groups of young unemployed sons would often take up this task for a community.

GUNNY SACKS OF PRIDE

The weather prediction for the weekend of November twenty-eight and twenty-nine of 1936 was bitter cold and windy with a threat of heavy lake effect snow on Monday. Therefore, a coal run along the tracks was needed immediately. Whoever could help was being asked to meet at Wusik's gas station on Saturday evening about 6:00 p.m., dress warm, bring lots of gunny sacks, flashlights and lanterns, and be prepared for an all-nighter on the tracks. If snow did come on Monday, it would be impossible to find coal, so Saturday and Sunday nights would be coal runs that would hopefully result in great hauls.

At 6:00 p.m. Saturday, it was ten degrees with a light wind that made it feel like ten below. Many young men from the community had dressed heavily. As bad as the weather was, it would only get worse. Therefore, no time to delay. They took off, heading for the southeast end of the coal run near Indianapolis Boulevard. They would then work their way back to Columbia Ave—three miles of track.

Others began trickling in, and by 7:15 there were twelve more guys dressed warm and ready to go. Sometime around 10:00 p.m., the first group came back looking half-frozen, but their sacks were full.

"How bad was it out there?"

"Really bitter!"

"When you guys get warmed up, Wusik's got a list of very cold neighbors for you to take these first loads of coal to. Kominski's have no coal at all, so two or three of you will need to build 'em a fire and get their furnace going. Oh, drink all of the coffee you want. Mr. Wleklinski and Mr. Guyeski came with a gift from the Polish National Alliance about 8:00 tonight, enough coffee to last us for two weeks if we're careful. They also gave us the names of two more families who have no heat." A portion of team one headed over to the Kaminskis on Ames Avenue. Kaminskis would be warm tonight.

Sunday, November 29th, continued to be cold and windy, but throughout that night coal was collected up and down the tracks. The collection area by three o'clock in the morning was extended to Hessville east and to the state line northwest. Everyone anticipated that snow would come by mid-day Monday, so collecting would need to be done before then. It remained bitterly cold. Finally, after 36 hours of continually collecting coal it was 6:00 a.m. Monday morning.

In Wusik's gas station, there was now a tired group of young men sitting on old chairs, on a rather rickety red table, and on the floor around a warm, pot-bellied stove, drinking half cups of coffee. They were all tired but not yet sleepy. Sleep would come, but right now they were together in good spirits—comrades in their own homemade locker room. They were poor and unemployed, but life had provided them with a full weekend's activities that required their youthful strength—a necessary and important performance that gave them pride. It was a pride that they could see in the eyes and smiling faces of one another and later would see in the eyes of grateful families and friends. But now they would just continue to laugh, talk, and sip their coffee.

None that early Monday morning would even notice the minuscule dots of the lake effect snow beginning to race past the picture window that gave its view of the early dawn over Columbia Avenue.

World War II had ended. Church bells rang and there was happiness everywhere. My grandmother (Busia) sent me down the alley to the butcher shop for three slices of baloney which we would have tonight for dinner to celebrate the ending of the war. I was just a kid, so I didn't understand rationing, nor how poor we were.

CATHERINE

That fall I started school at Saint Mary's, five blocks down the street. The building had been constructed in the 1870's. It had clapboard siding, very large windows, and no insulation. In winter you prayed that your seat was near the pot-bellied stove up front. Besides the four classrooms there was a large storage room upstairs that was seldom used except when the nuns took the seventh grade girls up there for a talk. Fifty yards from the school building on the edge of the gravel playground were the outhouses. You had to walk five feet down on the concrete stairs to get to the toilets and urinals. You ventured there only if you really needed to because the smell was nauseating, and it was not uncommon for a big kid to take any money you had.

In late fall of my fourth grade I met Catherine. I had seen her in class but we had never spoken. I was walking home when I saw four girls beating her up on the edge of the playground. They were pulling her hair, kicking, and spitting on her. She was crying, helpless and on her knees. I yelled and shooed them away. They screamed out that they would get her again. She then raised her head while tears streamed down her dirty face. I said "Why?" She just shrugged her shoulders and wept. She resisted my walking her hom, but I was hearing none of that. I wiped off her dirty face and found her books. I asked her, "Where's your coat?" She said. "I'm okay." I wrapped my coat around her. It was bitterly cold that afternoon. She said very little as we walked. When we got to her house—a one room apartment at the end of a row of eight other one room apartments, she opened the door. As I glanced in, even though I was a child, I recognized the gloomy frightening look of poverty, and the memory of that glance still haunts me today.

I told Busia everything. She listened and seemed to understand more profoundly than me. I learned later that Catherine's dad was killed at Iwo Jima and that her mom drank a lot. Soon Busia contacted some neighborhood ladies including Mrs. Jeblonowski from Kenwood Street, a seamstress. Together they made a coat, two dresses, and bought her new socks and shoes.

Two days before Christmas Busia and Mrs. Jeblonowski had Catherine and her mother over. They took Catherine into Busia's bedroom and helped her dress. When they came out I'm sure I had never seen a bigger smile on a little girl's face. Her mom just cried.

I often walked Catherine home after that, especially when it appeared that someone might try to hurt her. It got around that I was watching out for her.

As I reflect on those years, I recognize now that we didn't have much, but knowing Catherine made me understand that we really weren't poor. Someday I hope that the memory of my childhood glance of a very empty, depressing, dark room fades away. But if it means that I must also forget the biggest Christmas smile I have ever seen on a little girl's face, I'll keep the memories.

One very beautiful mid-October Friday, we left home and headed north to Evanston. Our two older sons were playing football on Saturday for Northwestern University. We got there around 5:00 p.m., did a bit of unpacking, and then headed downstairs to the hotel restaurant for a quiet meal. Outside the restaurant window we could see that the trees on both sides of the street were ablaze with their fall colors, and the evening touches of sunlight were performing magic with their leaves.

"Lord, When Did We See You?"

At meal's end my youngest son Tom and I headed outdoors for an evening walk. After going a fair distance, we turned the corner at McDonald's and found that the sidewalk was fairly crowded.

Out of the corner of my eye, I caught sight of a homeless man. He had his left hand out and cupped, while with his right hand he held together his lightweight, tattered, and zipper-less jacket. He was very unkempt, and next to him on the ground was a bundle tied together at the top with a stick. I found myself drawn to and looking directly at him as his eyes locked unswervingly on me in a deep and profoundly peaceful way. I remember at that moment saying to myself, "Why not, I can afford a buck or two."

I was sure I had some cash. I reached into my pocket and was pleasantly surprised. As I neared the homeless stranger, I pulled the cash out and looked into my right hand—a twenty dollar bill. I looked down at Tom. He didn't seem to know what was going on, so I slowly and somewhat shamefully pocketed the money. Then, Tom and I headed back toward the hotel. I remember affirming to myself:

"How can I give him a twenty? It's unreasonable. No one would expect me to give him a twenty." I tried to calm my conscience.

After our short walk back I reached into my pocket and then stopped dead in my tracks. The money was gone. I looked down at Tom and without explaining to him said, "Quick, Tom, we need to go back."

I knew we wouldn't find the money but I had to look. As we

walked quickly, I could see through the half-crowded sidewalk ahead of us the homeless guy coming our way. He was slowly waving his hand in the air. Soon I could hear him saying, "Sir, Sir, you dropped this." Crumpled in his waving hand was my twenty dollar bill. He continued, "I found it right after you left, but couldn't keep up with you and the boy."

As I looked into his eyes, I remembered why I had been compelled to look his way in the first place. It was his eyes. They were so deep, peaceful and caring—so calm and gentle. They belied the rest of his appearance. His eyes were not homeless at all.

Sheepishly, I said. "Sir, would you please keep the money?"

"Only if you really want me to."

"I do."

"Then I will."

He smiled a very quiet and calm smile, looked again into my eyes, then turned and walked away. Later I took a walk by myself. I looked for the man with eyes that seemed to calm me and bring me this strange peace. Though I searched for quite some time, I could not find him nor strangely, I could not find anyone who had seen him.

I never did find him. All I do know is that whoever he was, he was peacefully at home in our world. He was more at home than anyone I have ever met.

I ask still today, "Was it you, Lord", and is it we who are the homeless and needy wanderers.

Tuesday, October 22, 1935 was bitterly cold when Heinie and "Johnny Five" arrived at Wusic's gas station early that morning. They had promised old man Wusic that they would clean up before the station opened at 6:00 am.

BEING HUNGRY

Johnny started putting away chairs from a late Yellow Jacket semi-pro football team meeting the night before and Heinie busily swept around the gas pumps and entrance to the gas station. "Hey Heinie, How many games did Wolf say we had left this season?"

"Two. Calumet City and then two weeks later Chicago Heights."

Johnny said. "What's that you just uncovered in the grease with your broom? Here, let me get it."

"Nah, I'll get it, I'm sweepin."

"Well, what is it?" Heinie then said quietly while he rubbed off the grease, "It's a nickel."

"No s***, Here give it to me."

Heinie replied. "No, I picked it up."

"Yeah, but I saw it first."

Heinie, "Let's just say it's ours."

"Bull s***."

"Look, Johnny, I don't want to fight you for a nickel, but I will."

"OK, OK, it's ours. Well, what do you want to do with it?"

Heinie answered, "Well let's finish up and when old man Wusic gets here we'll go to the OK Bakery and buy a roll or a donut."

Within 15 minutes Mr. Wusic had arrived and Heinie and Johnny were taking a short, quick walk to the OK Bakery. "Hey, Heinie, what do you want to get?"

"A chocolate donut, they're easy to split and I love chocolate."

"Yeah, but it has a hole in the middle. Think of all you don't get when you buy a donut with a hole in the middle –all that empty space, and anyway I'm not that excited about chocolate."

Heinie asks, "Well, what do you want ?"

"Get some kind of roll filled with something like prune or raspberry or…" "OK, raspberry it is, but remember they're harder to break in half." "I know–we'll do it slow."

At this point they were 50 or so yards from the bakery, and already they could smell the freshly baked breads and pastries. They finally reached the bakery, opened the door, and were greeted by aromas that were pleasantly overpowering.

Toward the back of the bakery were two large ovens where bakers were moving breads in and out with gigantic flat wooden paddles. Smaller ovens were being used to prepare other baked goods like rolls and donuts.

Heinie and Johnny's purchase that morning would be only one item. They passed over the five cents, and then with a fresh raspberry filled roll in hand, they went out the side door of the bakery to sit on a nearby curb. Carefully, they broke the roll in half. This was accomplished to both of their surgical satisfactions. Each holding their share of the roll, they continued to enjoy the aroma. Finally, in silence they slowly, very slowly, ate their portion, saving a bit of raspberry filling for the last bite. They continued to sit there for a long moment, licking fingers for a taste of a roll that was no longer there.

Finally, Johnny, without looking up from his hands, said "Heinie?" "Yeah?" "I don't remember being this poor and hungry when we were kids."

Heinie simply shook his head and without looking up responded, "We weren't, Johnny, we weren't."

They then just sat together silently in the bitter cold. The experience of the taste of the roll they would long remember, but they would remember for an even longer time that they were still hungry–depression hungry.

It takes everything you've got—and then some.

Marion Was a Teacher

Marion's teaching career was varied. First she taught high school language arts, theatre, and typing. Later she taught in the elementary title I program, and secondary special education. Finally, she taught English composition and tutored college students in the university writing lab. Her career, periodically broken up as she tended to our growing family, spanned 30 years.

The following story occurred near the end of her career. I was a school superintendent and she was teaching high school in a nearby district.

It was a late fall Friday evening. I had gotten home around 5:30 p.m. She didn't arrive until about 6:30 p.m. I saw her pull up. She was slow getting out of the car, had no smile, and was carrying a load of papers and books in her arms. I opened the door and she said simply, "Let's go out and get some dinner somewhere."

Our drive to a favorite restaurant was silent. We arrived after the normal dinner hour so we were seated rather quickly. "Do you want to order?" "Not yet, just a cup of hot tea." Again after a long silence she said. "Ray, I want to tell you about my fourth period class."

Beginning with the first student she described all of the things that she knew about his childhood—the abuse, neglect, protective service involvement, and foster home care. Then she explained what she was attempting to do for this student on a daily basis. Next she told me about a second student, who was as needy—if not more needy—than the first. And again she explained what she was attempting to do during class in order to help this child. Then I heard story number three, story number four, and so on until there was a total of twelve such stories. When she finished she asked, "What do you think?" Somewhat overwhelmed, I recall saying, "I really don't know what to say."

"You see, Ray," she told me, "I don't have just twelve students in that class—I have thirty—but the immense needs of those twelve absorb all of my time, and I can virtually never get to the other eighteen sitting there patiently wanting to learn. I'm not even sure that what I am doing for the twelve is making any difference." She concluded with what has become an all-too-familiar phrase in education: "I don't know how much longer I can do this."

Marion really cared for her students. Nearly every teacher does, but there are conditions under which teaching becomes almost impossible. Most often these conditions are out of a teacher's control: poverty, deprivation, child abuse, neglect and daily hunger to name just a few.

An element of this story is often lost in the telling. The above story is focused on Marion's fourth period. Her teaching load that semester was five periods—as is the normal teaching load of all American high school teachers. We never did get to a discussion of any of her other teaching periods.

That evening we never did get to dinner either.

Friday was the end of the work week for the men of Pullman Standard and steel companies adjacent to this large plant.

"Rajmund, Go Get Your Dziadzia"

On a normal work day we would be looking for my grandfather (Dziadzia) to be home from work right around 4:20 p.m. If he wasn't home on paydays by 5:00 p.m. Busia, my grandmother, would begin pacing. By 5:20 I would hear, "Rajmund, go get your Dziadzia."

I would be out the door, through the back yard, past the chicken coup, down the alley, past the butcher shop, up the three-rounded concrete bar stairs, where I would then pull hard on the heavy wood door with the oval glass window prominently displaying the words, "Koch's Bar."

Once inside, the 18 foot dark wood bar was toward your right. Behind the bar beside Jack, the owner, himself, would be a set of large glass mirrors showing off an endless supply of whiskey bottles on glass shelving in front of the mirrors. The bar floor, like the bar itself, was hardwood, but looked as though it had seen hard times. There were round tables with chairs in the darker corners of the bar, but normally everyone stood or had elbow space at the bar itself. It wasn't a place where you sat and waited for someone to take your order—strictly a shot and a beer.

Whenever I came into the bar to do Busia's bidding, I drew the attention of at least a dozen or so of those closest to the door and Dziadzia whose spot was usually at the bar itself. Then I would be picked up and hugged or danced with by a couple of the bigger men like old man Pulkowski or Fyda. Finally, I'd be taken to a bar stool at the end of the bar in the corner farthest away from the door and given a bottle of coke with a straw. When in later years my brother Joe came with me, the shouts were louder, the dancing longer and then two stools and two cokes with straws. I knew most men in the bar for they were part of my everyday life as I walked the streets, shopped downtown, went for doughnuts, or just interacted in this close, extended family community.

Once in awhile, several of the younger men might be prompted by their older comrades to dance. A space in the middle of the barroom floor would be opened as men backed away and began clapping in unison providing the rhythmic beat for the Kazachok. Two or three young, very physically strong looking men would then roll up their sleeves, loosen their shirts and begin to dance. Often the dance would begin with the men linking their arms. Then quickly, the rhythm of the clapping would intensify as well as the foot-stomping and shouting. Eventually their dance would continue now from a full-squatted position with the kicking of alternate legs until competitors would give up and only one would remain. With a crescendo of shouting and clapping, it would be over and followed with a round of shots, beers, and salutes of "Nasdrovia."

Then the Busias would come in, sometimes in a small group. They would enter together, shouting at the men and at Jack, the bar owner. Dziadzia and other men would down their shots. Joe and I would be taken from our stools then hustled out of the bar and down the sidewalk.

We would all then head down the alley where Busia would continue her quite loud chastisement of Dziadzia as he sang and danced his version of the young men's dance down the now darkened alleyway.

At age 12, after school, Bobby and I would meet at the corner of Fields and Howard, throw our coats to the ground, and fight. Thirty or so kids would watch. Sometimes Bobby would win, sometimes I would.

WHO CAN JUDGE?

Afterwards, we would head to the coal yard, find a high pile to sit on, and talk. I learned a lot about Bobby those late afternoons. No dad, an alcoholic mom, and a grandfather who liked to use him as a punching bag. I had so much more, yet for all of our differences we were much alike—a couple of street kids who liked to fight and liked one another. Our neighborhood had lots of little stores, no end of bars, and only a few churches—mostly Catholic. Stealing was commonplace and many older guys were armed.

It was predictable that we would eventually plan something illegal. As fate would have it, the night it was planned for, my dad insisted that I drive with him to the north side of town to pick up a load of lumber. Bobby and three others were caught, arrested, and sent to boy's school. While at boy's school, Bobby got into very serious trouble and ended up in an adult security prison. We lost contact.

Eventually, I became a high school teacher. Our school decided to sponsor a program of delinquency prevention where penitentiary prisoners in shackles would present an auditorium session. That morning I sat with my class in the auditorium. The sound of the prisoners' shackles as they walked to the stage was eerie and frightening. The auditorium became deathly quiet except for that sound. The last prisoner hit me on the shoulder as he passed. I was stunned. As they presented, I strained to see if I could recognize him. Eventually, they finished and began their walk back. As the last prisoner got closer, I experienced a cold, overwhelming chill. It was Bobby—older, thinner and drawn, but Bobby. Guards gave us a moment in the back of the auditorium. Bobby asked about my dad and brother Joe. I could think of nothing except that I wanted to free him and run until we could hide together, safe in the coal yard. He sensed it and said, "Ray, it's OK. For some reason we are both where we need to be. Don't try to figure out why." He would forever be my friend.

The next day Juan Domingo, one of the toughest delinquent kids I have ever known came to my classroom. "I saw you talkin' to the con in the auditorium yesterday. How do I get in touch with him?" I told him and then he left.

Some 20 years later, I was sitting in my administrative office.

My secretary came in. "Dr Golarz, you have a call holding from a Captain Domingo, of narcotics operations, Chicago Police."

I answered and heard, "Bobby passed away in prison last night. Asked me if ever it happened, to make sure you knew."

"Thanks, Captain, thanks for calling."

"No problem, He redirected my life when I was young. I owe him like no other." He hung up.

I called my Dad and brother Joe. I asked them to meet me at old Saint Mary's Church to say a prayer for a street kid from the neighborhood. On my way to church, I drove past the coal yard then stopped momentarily at the corner of Fields and Howard. I rolled my window down. Through the heavy falling snow, my mind's eye could almost make them out—two street kids who liked to fight and who liked one another.

Who can judge the better life lived?

Over 150 years ago Horace Mann expressed his view of young women. He said that they would be perfect as teachers—bright, inexpensive and not permitted to marry. The die was cast. From that moment forward America would never understand the real cost of public education.

A National Shame

T hus, for those of you old enough to remember your teachers were: grade one: Miss ------; grade two: Miss ------; grade three: Miss ------ etc, etc. STRIKE ONE: THE ESTABLISHMENT OF A BASE OF INADEQUATE EDUCATIONAL FUNDING.

Years later, during the 1970s, the U.S. Supreme Court imposed on public schools the obligation to provide for the protection of students' personal rights, including freedom of speech. The assumption was that twelve to seventeen year-old students would recognize the difference between the legitimate exercise of rights and the abuse of such. The consequence of these Supreme Court actions required endless due-process hearings with witnesses and all legal provisions. I was responsible for setting up such a system in a large school district. Ultimately, the cost of all of these legal provisions, which included periodic moves to courts of appeal, was staggering—tens of thousands of dollars each semester. The more profound costs were the thousands of teacher and administrator hours taken from classroom instruction and the on-going need to hire substitutes to cover the absence of professional staff. This astounding obligation continues today. Teachers, understanding what it takes to remove a severely disruptive student, will often ignore significantly disruptive behavior. STRIKE TWO: FUNDS NEVER FOLLOWED THESE MANDATES.

Soon thereafter, public schools were mandated to include the full range of handicapped children. This is something that teachers had been supporting for years. But the mandate came with only the promise of funding. The best estimates of necessary funding being received still today is only 30%. Ask any parent in America the cost, time, and energy needed to care for one handicapped child for one day. If you get the whole story, It will astound you. Now consider the average teacher with possibly 10 or 15 of such children sprinkled daily throughout her classrooms. Remember, necessary financial support is at best 30%. Are you starting to get it? STRIKE THREE. ONLY A MODICUM OF SPECIAL EDUCATION FUNDING EVER FOLLOWED THE MANDATES.

But, the batter is still at the plate. You've not yet heard it all. Ask now what have we done to the learning environment of schools? Have we allowed for pockets of chaos—opening the door to a lack of order and civility? What crippling impact on the mental health of teachers and principals? For nearly 150 years America's public schools have been underfunded, overburdened and unjustly faulted. Yet they have continued to fight against these odds, including the indignations and erroneous designs of standardized testing. How can anyone who lives in this great land not see these injustices?

Our nation has not acted honorably. Instead, in the manner of the royalty on horseback in the movie "Braveheart," many of those empowered in our society shamelessly ride away. Then, once away from the battlefield, they audaciously and blatantly create an alternative school system not bound by the shackles bolted to the public system and its teachers. This very day this new system is being given legislative authorization and permission to siphon off the meager funds remaining in the hands of our first child—our American public schools.

My grandmother had finished her shopping downtown so we headed to the railroad tracks. The walk to our neighborhood along the tracks was two miles. There was a bus, but five cents per person could buy a loaf of bread.

DR. CONGREVE

The tracks were walked by the immigrants and Black Americans who made up our neighborhood. As I got older, I learned that we and our immigrant neighbors were just saving the nickel, whereas our Black neighbors were saving the nickel because, for them, a place on the bus was never guaranteed. It was not uncommon to see Black neighbors standing downtown on the side of the bus waiting for all of the whites to get on then hoping that there would still be room for them.

At age six, I was on a bus ride. As the bus traveled around the city, more passengers got on. Eventually the bus had standing room only. A big white man stopped directly in front of an elderly black woman seated across from me. I did not hear what he said, but she got up and he took her seat. It was soon clear that the moving bus was making her very unsteady. I got up and offered her my seat. She resisted but I made her sit. She smiled then nervously thanked me. We talked a little.

Months later, I spoke to my grandmother about these things. In her broken English, she said, "Rajmond, everyone poor in our neighborhood—no big shots. So we the Polish, Russians, Blacks and Jewish people, we take care of one another. It is not like this outside of neighborhood."

As I grew older I continued to see more and more systemic racism. I began to question our nation's resolve to stop it. Eventually, I became a young central office administrator in a large school district.

Our superintendent, Dr. Congreve, called me into his office and said, "Soon the NAACP will file a suit against us for racial segregation and discrimination. I'm putting you in charge of a team responding to interrogatories and seeking a defense." Week after week we worked, reviewing board minutes and district actions beginning with the year 1900. Half way through the task, I asked to meet with him.

"Dr. Congreve, we are only to 1948 but the actions and transcribed dialogue condemn the district in a hundred ways."

He responded, "I know, but complete your task thoroughly. Then bring me your findings."

I did as directed. Several months later he had me and my committee present our findings to him in public session. The prevailing reactions from much of the public as well as community leaders was "Let them sue us."

Dr. Congreve opted for a different and aggressive tack. He would force compliance upon the district by presenting to the board a plan for desegregation. With his public recommendation he would obligate agreement. If his plan were rejected, the courts could then direct compliance.

Soon after, he fell desperately ill and was hospitalized. From his hospital bed he directed us to publicly present his plan. We did and his plan was adopted. Soon thereafter he died. We lost a leader of courage and conviction and one we had come to admire. He taught us much. He especially taught us that white Americans like him must stand shoulder to shoulder with Black Americans if we intend to secure justice. Eradication of racial discrimination will only occur if we first commit to what we know is right and just and then have the courage to act.

Today, particularly, we must act.

I went to a small college in East Chicago. The registration desk was near the front door. Any conversations you had would not be private.

CLOSE TO THE BLESSED
VIRGIN'S ALTAR

So when Michael entered dressed in his three piece olive green wool suit and bowler hat there would be no confidentiality. He had come to enroll. Eventually the clerk (Kathy) assisting his enrollment asked him about his preferred course of study. He laid his bowler hat on the counter and replied. "I'm here to initiate a Ph.D. program." The dean came over and said, "Son, this college offers only a bachelor's degree program," At which Michael responded, "Well, then I assume you can get me started." We had a new freshman college classmate.

Michael lived alone in an upscale rental apartment two blocks from our college. His payment in full for his college fall semester was no fluke, he always had money. Furthermore, his olive green suit was only one of many elegant outfits. Despite his obvious idiosyncrasies, we liked him. There wasn't a matched pair in our motley class, so he fit. We came to like him so much that he was given a nickname, "Duke." In those days, when you were given a nickname, you were considered "in." Duke was a quiet guy who seemed to prefer being alone. Tom Sertich (Bull), one of our South Chicago classmates would have none of that and would drag Duke to places he didn't really want to go. Bull wasn't a guy you could resist.

On Sundays when we played pick-up football games at Kosciuszko Park, Bull would often bring Duke. Duke would never play but somehow he seemed to like being there. Only once did he even touch the ball. An out of bounds punt came right at him and he caught it.

He seemed really surprised and pleased. We cheered. It was as if he had never caught a football before. At season's end, Bull bought little three inch high trophies at Woolworths. Everyone got one, including Duke.

Winter break, just after Christmas, Bull and several classmates from South Chicago came to my house during a massive snow storm. They struggled to get it out. Duke had committed suicide. It was the foul odor in the hallway that prompted the police to go into his room. They found him lying on his bed decked out in his olive suit. He died of some kind of overdose, but he left no note. In his right hand he held his little three inch high trophy. Bull was impossible to console.

There was no funeral. Someone from Boston claimed his body. The next week Bull went to the police department. A police officer friend of his gave him Duke's little trophy. In our first class after winter break we couldn't get past Duke's empty chair. We hadn't even spoken yet to one another about our deepest pain—the pain you feel when a loved one commits suicide. Should we have known what he was planning?

No one talked about church, no one suggested. But all twenty-five of us without speaking left our books in class and walked the three blocks to Assumption church. Bull found the pastor and asked if he had a nice place for a little trophy. Father said, "Was it Duke's?" Bull nodded. Father smiled and then told us, "You know Duke never knew his mom, and though he was not Catholic he liked to come here and sit in the first pew close to the Blessed Virgin's altar—how about if we put his trophy there?"

We all then knelt together near that altar leaving one empty seat.

We sat silently until only the red vigil light near the main altar and the little votive candles gave soft light to the comforting and darkening church.

My dad was a steelworker—a second helper working an Open Hearth furnace. Second helpers were the work horses shoveling various metals into the furnace for the entire eight hour shift. Occasionally the furnace of bubbling metals would "Spit "and molten steel would explode into the air and rain down in marble sized pellets. These molten falling pellets would cut through clothing, run down your back and occasionally get stuck in your belt area where they left open wounds in your lower back.

"Last Full Measure"

As a young child I once saw my dad without his shirt. I saw the bright red long fresh wounds. I wanted to cry. He dropped to one knee, put his hands on my shoulders and said "It's OK son." But for me it never was. I didn't relax until he had his own open hearth furnace and could select his team.

From the labor gang he picked a man he really respected, nicknamed "Pea Shoot." The first time I met Pea Shoot he was sitting with dad on the back steps of our house having coffee. He was a former WWII navy guy who had muscles everywhere. Dad had to go in for a bit so we got a chance to talk. I asked him about Omaha Beach. He laughed and told me that he had been a sailor on a ship. I asked if he had gotten medals. He again laughed and said that he had given them to my dad because he didn't have a safe place to keep them. Pea Shoot was easy to talk to and easy to like. Over time we didn't have many interactions but they were always upbeat.

It wasn't until years later that I began to know more about Pea Shoot. It started as I unintentionally caught bits and pieces of dad's conversations with mom. It culminated with a long after mid-night talk at the kitchen table with dad. "Everything okay, Dad?" "Sit with me in the kitchen, son." I listened as he talked for hours.

I had no idea that Pea Shoot was in the fight of his life with alcoholism. Didn't know that Dad had taken him to AA meetings. Didn't know that the nightmares and night sweats from the war had never ended. Didn't know that Pea Shoot had given Dad his medals for fear that he might pawn them for a bottle. Didn't know that the mysterious phone calls to Dad over the years were pleas from Pea Shoot's wife to please help find him. Didn't know that Dad knew to look first for Pea Shoot in the alleyways of the Harbor bars. Didn't know that he covered for Pea Shoot when he didn't report for work. I had known none of these things. "What can I do, Dad?" "Pray for him son. He and those like him have given to our country their last full measure. They deserve our never ending admiration and respect."

Finally, one afternoon Dad got the call. Pea Shoot was dead. Found by the police beaten and killed in a Harbor alleyway. Dad went with mom into his bedroom. I could hear him weeping bitterly.

Several days later Dad went into his bedroom and came out with several medals—two Purple Hearts and the Navy Cross. "Please come with me, son." At the funeral home, with Pea Shoot's wife, Dad pinned the medals on Pea Shoot. Then with his hand laid gently on Pea Shoot's chest, he said quietly, "Rest now, good friend. You're home." He then backed away and slowly saluted.

We drove home in respectful silence.

The steel processing plant was on Marble Street. It had been twelve years since I had seen a co-worker in that plant get his arm crushed in a press up to his elbow. As I turned now onto the street, I could still clearly recall his screams. God, how we all had wanted him to pass out.

MARBLE STREET

N ow, however, having completed college and a master's degree
I was back on Marble Street. I was a young administrator in
charge of a newly formed poverty prevention program. No longer did
I wear metatarsal work boots, stuff work gloves in my back pocket,
or carry a metal lunchbox—all had been replaced by a white shirt
and tie.

In those bygone years, I had never noticed the row of run down,
unpainted houses across the street from the steel plant. I would now
soon be walking down a half flight of concrete stairs into one of
several basement apartments in a dilapidated 1880 structure.

With me was Fred. Fred was head of intervention services for the
inner city. He was formidable—a six foot three, 240 pound, barrel-
chested powerhouse. We were on the hunt for a reported twelve-
year- old girl with no adult care or supervision who had been spotted
foraging for food in garbage cans. We got to a door in the darkened
area at the bottom of the stairs. Fred knocked. No response. The
door was slightly ajar so Fred pushed it open. Immediately roaches
scurried everywhere. One step in and we were overwhelmed by the
smell of rot, decay, vomit, and urine.

Acclimating to the dark, we could now see movement on the
floor in the corner of the room. Cowering there was a half-clad, very
thin, and dirty little girl. She was clearly terrified. Fred, the father
of children that age stood there as tears streamed down his face.
He then declared in defiant terms, "This isn't happening. This is not

going to happen." Within a half hour we had secured a police car with a female officer. She wrapped the child in a heavy blanket and then put her into the back seat of the squad car. Fred and I followed as they moved through traffic on the way to the Department of Public Welfare, Gary office. Once there, things continued to move quickly. Emergency custody was secured and with Fred's assistance we got temporary placement at the Mayflower Home for Girls.

We left the girl with Department of Public Welfare authorities and got into our car. Fred said "We have just one more thing to do before we get to the Mayflower House. Wait for me as I run into this Sears department store." He came out with a fairly good sized bag. "Fred, what's in the bag?" "I have girls this age. They don't sleep well unless they can wrap their arms around a nice soft doll."

The Mayflower house became a permanent placement. Mrs. King in the high school book store became the unofficial surrogate mother. Time moved on, as it always does, and newly neglected and abused children became our focus.

Years later I was teaching a college course to Chicago police officers. After class, a young officer stopped me and said, "Dr. Golarz, my wife's a cop like me and works the inner city here in Chicago—she handles neglected kids. She asked me to ask you if you remember Marble Street." "'Sure I do." "Well, she wanted you and Mr. Fred to know that she still has that doll he gave to her."

When I first met Dr. Emily Garfield, she was conducting conferences on drug prevention. In her earlier years after graduating Stanford with highest honors, she had applied to medical school. Though she met all qualifications, she was ultimately advised that medical school would not be available to her, a woman.

AT WHAT POINT RESPECT?

As a teacher, one of my assignments was to coach track. After school, my team gathered in their track attire—boys, that is. Girls watched from the sidelines. I was having trouble finding a 100 yard dash competitor. As practice concluded, one of the girls cornered me and said, "Mr. Golarz, Cynthia is really good at that dash thing you're trying to get someone to do." So, I said "Cynthia, come here and line up with these guys." Fifty middle-school boys and girls spread along the sidelines. I had never seen a middle-school child run so fast—boy or girl. I initiated a girl's track team immediately. When I left that school, tragically the girls' track team was discontinued.

I was a young administrator attending a corporate meeting, when I overheard a conversation between two older male members of the group. "Listen Eddie, I respect your moral position. But if we promote a woman to this level and she becomes pregnant and consequently must miss critical corporate meetings, where are we then Eddie? Where are we then?"

When I was superintendent of schools, we opened a parent center in a poverty community, I asked the principal, Nancy, "How early do these young mothers come to this center?" "By 6:00 a.m. They would get here at 5:00 a.m. if we were open." "Why, Nancy?" "In early mornings, their drunken boyfriends or husbands come home from the bars looking for them. What then happens throughout this community can only be described as rape."

I reviewed the salaries of all administrators. I found that women administrators were receiving on average $10,000 less than men performing the same duties. The next board meeting I brought a recommendation for wage increases sufficient to create equity. One board member asked, "Are these excessive raises really necessary?" I replied, "Well, would you prefer a court order for past due wages?"

In a casual conversation about good places to golf, an acquaintance of mine mentioned a course I wasn't familiar with. I said, "Jack, I don't know that course." He responded casually, "Really, it's one of the finest—very private, no women, of course."

When Hillary Clinton was running for president, reporters were interviewing a cross section of prospective voters. When questioning began to focus upon the difference between the qualifications of male versus female, one man crystallized the consensus view. "Here's how it is. Mama runs the kitchen—but I own the house."

I have had close male friends in my life. But, if I had ever regarded any of them in the ways described above, our friendship would have ended and there would be no coming back. I would have violated the trust that friends silently grant to one another—respect. Unless we come to understand that women must be respected as equals, the time will come when they too will surely not see a way back.

In my youth I boxed. My father told me, "Son, if you are ever in a match where it is clear you could injure your opponent, stop. To destroy another person's dignity is never the measure of true strength." Had I asked if this applied to my interaction with women, he would have smiled and then said, "Really, what do you think, son?"

As we leave childhood somehow we slowly slide into needing and deserving more things—the pretty things, the trip to the Riviera, the cruise, the updated kitchen, the finest wines and most expensive restaurants. Further, we convince ourselves that these things are what we need and deserve—as Sally said in the Christmas Film, **A Charlie Brown Christmas***, "All I want is my fair share."*

ONE OF GOD'S FAVORITE PLACES OVER THE TRACKS

I s the time of the simple joys of our childhood too far away—only a vague memory? Did the years slowly bury our longing for our once treasured "Rosebud"?

I grew up three houses from a long and narrow empty field above which were high electrical wires. The wires were held up by enormous sixty-foot steel structures that had the appearance of a parade of giant robots.

We named this field "The Weeds." The far end of this field bordered the railroad tracks. The field itself had never been leveled therefore, the ground was unspoiled. Many rocks, small gullies, an array of trees, wild flowers and prairie grasses were everywhere. It was alive with creatures and bugs of all kinds. Our parents permitted us to play in "the weeds." Never, never, however, were we to leave the weeds and venture over the railroad tracks.

Alas, in the manner of Adam and Eve we didn't listen, It didn't take long for us to sin and enter the "forbidden lands and taste of its fruits." Long ago, over these tracks, there had existed small long bodies of water known as the Finger Lakes. Sadly, landfills, and the constructing of warehouses, factories, and roads had all but eliminated the existence of these pristine lakes and the flora and fauna that surrounded them. What remained was but a shadow of that forgotten place. Yet anyone who explored this remaining sanctuary with a child's imagination could share a scene that frontiersmen must have found in every part of our virgin country before man conquered and civilized the wilderness.

The trees around the now smaller remaining Finger Lakes area were larger than the trees found in "The Weeds." The prairie grass flowers were of a wider array and their colors more intense. As we approached, animals of all kinds that had been comfortably sunning dove for the protection of the waters. These remaining little lakes were clear and were four to five feet deep. Along the edges were hundreds of tadpoles. The sand was white beach sand, for this area had in its distant past been the shore of Lake Michigan. Thousands of these treasure spots still remain across our country. They are missed or forgotten by most adults. We see only a muddy pond, or a dirty, wet place at the end of the railroad tracks where the eyes of little children, as we all once were, see the treasure. Because of their childhood innocence these places call to them to come, splash, touch, and play.

Though I was always captivated when I ventured into these forbidden lands, it was my little sister Barbara who seemed most taken. Often as her smiling face looked up from her bare-footed squatting position at water's edge she would ask, "Ray, is this one of God's favorite places?" "Yes," I would reply. "I knew it, I knew it. I knew it. It's mine too, Ray. It's mine too." Then overflowing with joy, and using her little child's fingers, she would gently stroke the water and watch the tadpoles scurry to different places—places I'm sure that only she and God talked about.

So, my grown-up friends, risk once more. Close your eyes, picture water's edge, breathe deeply, then barefooted, find again that "just a moment ago place" that is yours alone.

Your "Rosebud" is not forever lost—it has simply been temporarily mislaid.

Back in the day there was only one grade on your report card that parents wanted to see—conduct. Heaven help the child who had anything other than an A. But sadly, things have changed.

It's Not Math or English That Must Be the Essential Studies

Mrs. Riley was a 16 year veteran teacher. She taught seventh grade. One of her pupils refused to sit in her assigned seat then screamed out. "You can't make me, b****." She then ran to the classroom door and began repeatedly opening then slamming it. The deafening sound could be heard throughout the entire wing of the school. Mrs. Riley could not get her to stop. Several additional students normally well behaved, distraught by this noise began running in the room and screaming at the top of their voices. The bedlam went on for 25 minutes—an eternity for Mrs. Riley. It took a full half hour for her intercom requests for assistance to result in help. By that time control in her classroom had totally deteriorated.

Mrs. Riley hadn't planned to leave teaching but this was the eighth significant incident this semester and it was only November. Last year there were six of these travesties for the entire year and that seemed intolerable. More and more of her students seemed to have little or no understanding of civil behavior. She resigned at semester's end. She lasted longer than most. Forty percent of new teachers, for these reasons, leave within five years.

Mr. Edison, high school coach, was greeting students as they were entering the building. Up the stairs came J.B. Mr. Edison said "Good morning J.B." J.B. responded "Go f*** yourself." Dr. Shelly Wick, new principal, observed the incident. Edison said," Did you hear that? She replied, "Mr. Edison, you don't understand the young man's background. That was his way of saying 'Good Morning.' And further, he has his free speech rights."

During the Casey Anthony trial, a young man gestured his isolated middle finger at one of the attorneys. A visibly agitated Judge Perry called the young man to the bench "Did you see the sign as you came into the courtroom expressly forbidding gestures or audible comments showing approval or disapproval." "Yes your honor." The young man was then fined and sentenced to six days in the Orange County Jail.

No one is suggesting that disruptive students who ignore the rights of others be jailed. However, classrooms and schools must be treated no differently than courts of law in session. They cannot be the practice fields for the learning of personal rights and freedoms. If individual rights are to be learned in school, civility and respect for others must be first taught and repeatedly practiced.

Occasionally, my wife and I go to an opera or live staged performance. Any significant disruption during those magnificent performances would ruin or destroy the presented art.

Forty years of research attest to the need for a relaxed and calm atmosphere within classrooms and schools in order to maximize learning. This cannot occur unless classroom teachers can exercise immediate control over their classrooms. Anything less erodes order. Teacher authority is imperative and parental support along with parental modeling is critical.

The foundations of a democratic society are first civility and respect. A generation without these skills and understandings will quickly move us toward anarchy for they will have never understood that their rights can never supersede the rights of the many. In order to sustain a viable classroom, school, or a nation's democracy, the common good must always triumph over individual rights.

Uncle Andy in his army uniform and Uncle Ed in his navy uniform were taking turns hoisting me onto their shoulders. The war was over and they were home.

COPS

Years later, at Christmas dinners I would look admiringly at them both as they participated in the night before Christmas feasts, dressed then in their police uniforms. Andy made captain first, followed shortly thereafter by Ed. They were, for our entire ethnic community, a source of continuous pride. They never spoke to us of their police work, but then again they never spoke of their experiences at Omaha Beach or Okinawa.

After teaching and coaching for five years, I headed up a federal criminal justice delinquency prevention effort. For the next twelve years, I worked the streets with regular police and narcotics officers. In the courts, probation and parole officers became my close friends. During those years, I never met a "bad cop." Once, in a meeting in the Chief's office, a very young- looking police officer who had been serving as an undercover agent in my project reported that he had taken three swats from the assistant principal in order to affirm his delinquent identify. Then, teasing me, he said "Ray, after my undercover duty, and I'm back in a squad car, don't speed while driving through my part of town."

Later, I became president of the Indiana Chapter for the prevention of child abuse. This is where I experienced the most profound and deepest commitment of police. I cannot even write about the cases we dealt with. Describing these would create images of such horror that anyone who read about them would never be able to forget. Man's inhumanity to little babies is the worst of all sins, and the cops I knew dealt with it all. During these times I saw young officers, parents themselves, weep. Those I worked with took their commitment to protect and serve seriously. Sadly, I watched many of them push too hard, struggle with addictions, attempt suicides, and lose close ties to their own families.

Eventually, I taught law enforcement officers in the Chicago land area. I taught psychology, including theories of deviant behavior. Each semester for ten years, I would have 80 to 100 in each of my classes. They were young men and women officers, representing virtually every ethnicity and race in Chicago. They were the most intense of students. As I lectured you could hear a pin drop. They were ever so focused—so intent on knowing. They were particularly interested in techniques to deal with deviant behaviors. In retrospect, why would they not? They lived daily where not knowing might cost them their lives. I miss those classes—the moments of levity and dialog exchanges that relived, for a moment, the heavy burdens they carried.

Today's world has now grown dark. Those who protect our streets, and communities have been cast as vile enemies—not poverty, not inequality, not systemic racism, but rather our sons and daughters who opted to become cops and have never forgotten their oath to protect and serve and do so on a modest income that would surprise most.

Remember always that beneath their blue uniform they are "us" and like us they don't respond well to being spit upon, needing to duck from a bottle thrown or maced with bear spray. Are they perfect? No. But then, clearly, neither are we. Do we want them to resign, retire early, or simply not respond to calls in potentially dangerous situations?

Consider, fellow Americans, what you disassemble or defund.

I grew up in a poor neighborhood near the south side of Chicago. The neighborhood was ethnically and racially mixed—Polish, Blacks, Jewish and Russians.

RACIAL HATRED—AMERICA'S ACHILLES HEEL

F ights were common. Sometimes they were white on white, or white on black, or Jewish on Russian. Usually, after a good fight, we would all head for the coal yard, sit together on a high pile of coal and share a smoke. We had a vague sense of ethnic and racial injustice, but the neighborhood tended to temper that. If you, a white kid, came home after being whipped in a fight by some black kid, it would be tough running around screaming racial slurs when your grandmother was sitting in the back yard with two neighborhood black grandmothers engaged in pleasant conversation.

Eventually, I became a young central office school administrator. I observed discrimination and racism first hand. I saw racist hiring practices, denial of access, and discriminatory housing practices. During this time we got a new superintendent Dr. Arthur. He was committed to addressing these discriminatory issues. He did so first by changing district hiring and promotion practices. He followed with district-wide seminars focused on racism and racial injustices. During these workshops, we were exposed to realities about racism that we had never known. The existence and pervasiveness of systemic racism became crystal clear.

The atmosphere in many workshops became tense. Many older, white male teachers resented the workshops. Some walked out. As the workshops continued, those who stayed were introduced to "Miss Ann" the bane of Black men. We reviewed research exposing the relationship between discrimination of women and racial discrimination, and how racial stereotyping entered our classrooms.

Soon afterwards, while Dr. Arthur was at a meeting, persons using shotguns fired at his home through his living room and bedroom windows. His children and wife were home. He met with several of us the next morning. He was shaken and asked if we thought these perpetrators might be from out of town. We advised him that we thought not. Rather, we believed that they lived within the city in all white neighborhoods. He resigned shortly thereafter.

Our next superintendent inherited an NAACP suit for discrimination that had been 80 years in the making. Tragically he died prematurely. However, he lived long enough to successfully put into place a desegregation plan.

Worse days followed. Several years later a racial war between two segregated neighborhoods spilled over into two inner city high schools. By day's end squad cars from as far away as Chicago were needed to regain control of the streets and classroom hallways. We looked up from the boundaries of our own community and saw that we were not alone. We were living part of a national tragedy.

A restless calm settled for a time over our country. But now, over these past five years the scab slowly forming over our nation's long standing racial wound has been viciously torn off, and we again profusely bleed.

I sat today at my desk and gazed into my back yard. If I looked long and hard enough I could see three grandmothers engaged in pleasant conversation. Were they, in that moment, on the right path? Are we, their children, now individual glaciers of ice on an ocean drifting again away from one another? Is there no possible way back? What if we force ourselves to truly believe and then create that elusive peaceful time? It is, after all, as with our grandmothers, still in our hands. And if we refuse, then what hope is there for us and our posterity? How will that posterity look back at us?

It was a beautiful fall Saturday afternoon when I went into the office to wrap up some loose ends. Within minutes of arriving the phone rang.

GOD'S GUIDING HAND

"Ray, this is Jack, Superintendent of Hillside. Last night at the conclusion of the football game between your school district and mine, Mr. Harrison, one of your veteran coaches, was, in full view, urinating on the front tire of one of our buses as our cheerleaders and their parents were boarding. Several in the crowd told him to stop, but he simply continued, yelled some obscenities, fell, and then wandered off. I thought you needed to know." I thanked him then made some calls. What I heard was that he was often publically drunk, involved in many bar fights and the best damn soccer and track coach in the state.

Afterwards, in executive session with my school board I was advised to tread carefully. Soon thereafter, a coalition of coaches asked to see me. Pressure was mounting to just give him a slap on the wrist. That seemed a no brainer, but something kept bothering me. It was as if I was being guided. The next morning I met with the coach. He seemed genuinely remorseful. I could have ended the whole thing with a "Don't do it again," but for some reason I said, "I may suspend you from coaching—not sure yet. I will let you know." He left and I sat there still uncertain. Eventually, the pressure mounted, including a crowd in front of the administration center with signs—"save our coach. " I was reaching a weak point when I got the following call.

"Dr. Golarz?"

"Yes."

"This is Dr. Jones from the alcoholic rehab center. Our patient,

Coach Harrison has given us permission to talk to you. Dr. Golarz, you are the first person who has gotten his attention in nine years."

"Are you saying not to punish him?"

"My God, no. If there are no consequences again for his actions he will assuredly drink himself to death within one or two years. Need I say more?"

"No Doctor, thank you."

The next morning I had Coach Harrison in my office. "Coach this meeting will be brief. Your behavior warrants dismissal from coaching for the remainder of your career. But I think your 20 years of exemplary coaching requires that we take a different approach. If you can stay alcohol free for a full year and your doctors can so testify then you will be back coaching. Fair?"

"Very fair, thank you."

That afternoon I met with Coach Tony, the representative of coaches. "Tony, I have heard that besides your successful coaching you are respected particularly for your ethics on and off the field. May I ask you a couple of questions?"

"Sure."

"If the doctor of your star player confidentially called you and advised you that if you played him it would likely kill him. Would you play him?"

"Of course not."

"What if you were the only one who knew this?"

"Wouldn't matter."

"Well, coach, I have a star player I can't play because …"

"You don't have to say anymore Dr. Golarz. You won't get any trouble from coaches."

Several months later I was visited by a young lady. "Dr. Golarz, you don't know me. Nine years ago when Coach Harrison's daughter was dying in children's hospital, I was her roommate. We talked a lot. She is not here to say this to you, so I'll say it for her. Thanks for taking care of my dad."

Coach Harrison, by God's grace, coached honorably for the next 15 years.

One percent of the population of the United States controls 40% of the wealth. Further, nearly 20% of the nation's children, mostly white, live in poverty. These staggering facts result in massive pockets of undereducated, hopeless, hungry and angry human beings.

How About We Stop Blaming Cops

W here these people reside you find high crime rates, child and domestic abuse, drug abuse and despair. They live in isolated neighborhoods. Therefore, those who are better off seldom see them unless shopping at Wal-Mart, Goodwill or the Dollar Store. America's polite society ignores the primary causes of their plight and blames them. The poor are resented and they feel it. Consequently, often their reaction to outsiders is mistrust, anger, and resentment.

The only ones we send into their neighborhoods are cops and occasionally the staff of a federally funded program. I headed up one of those programs with a staff of thirty-five. We lived in those pockets of despair, breathed the same foul air, and provided emergency shelter, a winter coat, some food, and a lot of empathy. We kidded ourselves that we were making a difference as we bandaged everything that we could. Daily coming back to unpredictable and challenging emergencies was numbing.

During my fifth year, child and domestic abuse during the winter months had become even more brutal. The worst was when I found a baby too late. His breathing was shallow and labored. He died of dehydration and exposure the next morning, despite the police and hospital's best efforts. In another case the parent had broken many of the infant's bones and was planning to submerge the baby's legs into boiling water to burn out the devil. The month went on and on like that.

Soon thereafter, I was in a Calumet City bar/restaurant, meeting with narcotics officers, Mickey, Nick, and Andy, planning a county wide drug intervention. I hadn't been feeling well, nerves maybe, didn't know. Nick and Andy noticed. After the meeting, I had but one call waiting—another suspected child abuse. As I was leaving, Nick said, "Ray, you OK?" I replied, "Thanks, OK."

The house was another unrepaired rental. The front porch was without several floorboards, snow and ice hid some of the additional holes. I knocked. The door slowly opened. But no one was there. I yelled. No response. I yelled again. I could hear a baby whimpering. The inside of the house revealed many missing floorboards and holes in the walls. The smell of urine, and defecation was overpowering and nauseating. In a bathtub filled with soiled dippers I found him, an infant with little clothing, shivering and coughing. Though I resisted, my mind instantly went to similar recent experiences.

I reached for the child but my arms wouldn't respond. I forced intensely but than began to shake uncontrollably. I couldn't stop. At that moment Nick appeared from out of nowhere. He put his hand gently on my back and said. "We'll take it from here Ray." I don't remember all of it. Nick and Andy took me and the infant into a car. I sat there shaking. "Nick, what's wrong with me?" "You hit the wall Ray—hit it hard. You've got to back away now. We and your people will cover for ya. We've all been where you are. Relax now."

Police officers respond to traumatic calls daily—child abuse, intense violence, homicides and brutality of every kind. They virtually never tell their families. Their repeated exposure invariably causes mental illness, alcoholism, PTSD and suicide. As a society, we have allowed the monsters of poverty, hopelessness, and deprivation to grow out of control in neighborhoods throughout America. Then when predictable crises occur we send police and a small handful of others in and say, "Make it go away."

The fact that our police officers do this for ten or twenty years should be viewed as nothing less than miraculous.

My childhood neighborhood was made up of Black Americans and Polish, Russian, and Jewish immigrants. We were a mixed bag but we had a commonality—the neighborhood.

WE CAN NO LONGER REMAIN YANKEES AND REBELS

At age 20 I got a job working with mostly young men from the Deep South: Louisiana, Mississippi, and Alabama. The steel foundry that brought us together was a low-paying non-union plant near Chicago. The plant's massive presses were notorious for taking off workers fingers, hands and occasionally arms. Oily grime was everywhere as well as rats that didn't run from you. The Southern boys, with their confederate flags and guitar singing at lunch time, were pervasive throughout the plant. They were mostly 17 to 22 years old, had dropped out of school, were married and had one or two kids.

Only once did several of us interact with them socially. It was after work on a Friday pay-day. We met at Stan's Bar next to the B&O tracks. One of the Southern boys put his entire pay into a pin-ball machine while the remainder of us proceeded to drink too much As we were leaving, one of them shouted a cheer for Robert E. Lee and with gusto the rest chimed in. Another then screamed out praise to the bartender for not allowing N****** in the bar. Such disparaging comments throughout the evening plus the end of the night salutes made it clear that they were still engaged in the Civil War. We, the sons of immigrants, felt a palpable discomfort. We had been raised in neighborhoods attempting inclusion. In this atmosphere, we were more than uncomfortable. The evening had become frightening.

Some months later I got a laboring job at the enormous U.S. Steel plant. Within its massive roofed structures were polished concrete floors extending fifty yards to your left and right and several hundred yards ahead of you. One hundred and fifty feet above were massive cranes carrying 50,000 pound coils of steel to load onto flatbed trucks. The sounds were always deafening. The entire plants work force of 30,000 was under the protection of the AFL-CIO union. Safety dominated everything. Workers were of every race and ethnicity and foreign languages were heard as often as English. We routinely mixed when interacting or eating lunch. Isolating by race or ethnicity was not very common. Further, you learned very quickly, that in such social settings there were strict unwritten rules prohibiting racial or ethnic slurs. Violating such rules was not tolerated.

For me, the differences between the experiences of the steel foundry and the U.S. Steel plant were stark. It was as the experience of the Joad family in the movie, *The Gropes of Wrath*—moving from the experience of inhumane camps of decadence to the civilized and respectful experience of the government run facilities. U.S. Steel was by no means a perfect world but the union, management, and fellow workers seemed to be trying to make it that way. It wasn't just the emphasis upon cleanliness and safety. It was so much more. There was an emphasis upon getting along and working in groups of mixed races and ethnicities whenever possible.

Organizations and nations of viability insure their viability because they refuse to segregate. Hate and segregation cripple what they could be. To be committed to the "dream" of this nation, we must in every workplace, school, and community always be, "We the People." There can be no compromising. The risk is too great to the democracy itself. The war must end. It's time to drop arms, let them rust in the fields, and head home.

On the kitchen table of a farm in Oklahoma, a boy of the Choctaw tribe was born. He would become a warrior and be my friend. His name was Don Sims.

CHOCTAW WARRIOR—AMERICAN EDUCATIONAL LEADER

I first met Don at a conference in Phoenix. Rarely had I met anyone so enthusiastic. We talked until early morning about ways to help children. He then invited me to his reservation and Riverside Indian School in Oklahoma.

On my first visit he took me to a large empty field near the center of the reservation. He then said, "Ray, there will be a basketball gym here, and shortly thereafter my Indian students will honor themselves in the basketball state tournament." I said, "When do you start construction?" He laughed and said, "Don't know yet, don't have the money." Six years later, the Riverside Indian students went to the final four.

On another occasion he called me at 1:00 am in the morning. Half awake, I heard, "Ray, I've' got an Idea. I'm going to purchase from *USA Today* 450 daily newspapers. Each of the newspapers will have the name and address of each kid on this campus. Virtually none of my kids have ever seen their name in print nor been given anything that was theirs alone." On my next visit, the campus was a treasure to behold. Over 150 students were visible throughout the campus reading "their" *USA Today*.

The dropout rate in Indian schools is horrific. Don's school was no exception. So he started a school for dropouts. But unlike other dropout schools his school was different. There would be no failures. There would be no semesters or other such traditional barriers. Each enrolled student would take whatever time they needed in each course of study. In its first year, Don's school graduated over 100 students.

After Riverside, Don accepted the challenge of Sherman Indian School in California, a school representing students from over 80 Native tribes. By Don's second year he and his teachers made a modification to the report card. The report card would have a new grade designation. NY (not yet). Failure would not be an option.

Several years later Don created and then held on campus a first of its kind—an all tribes Powwow. Around the evening fire, the children and many chiefs of the Sioux, Navaho, Fox, Cherokee, Apache, and many others danced in their traditional attire. As the fire waned, the princess of the powwow was selected. Don, with permission of tribal elders, asked that I dance with her. It was for me an honor and now a treasured memory.

My visits became more infrequent but always so very uplifting for whenever arriving at his office, it was always filled with native students. I asked him once of this unusual openness and he simply replied, "They need this and, I guess, so do I." Then finally in one last phone conversation the first seven minutes or so, he seemed very distant and confused as to my identity. Finally, for no apparent reason, he excitedly exclaimed, "Ray!" We talked only a bit more. I hung up understanding that I would not be talking to my friend again in this lifetime. I sat in silence.

In earlier years we half jokingly kidded that when we neared the end of this life we would go to Eagle Nest Butte and share a pipe. I would have liked that, I believe he would have too. The Choctaw recognize death only as a new journey. So I say. "Journey on good friend, be in harmony with nature, and be with **Nanishta.** We will try to follow the path here that you left for us. It is a path of honor."

By noon my brother Joe, age 10 and I, age 12 had finished our first round of caddying, eaten our baloney sandwiches, and were starting a game of mumblety-peg. Some 30 yards behind us, older caddies were running toward a group that was forming. There appeared to be some kind of fight.

THE BEAUTY AND POWER
OF COMPASSION

F inally a break in the crowd allowed us to see, though not clearly.
One big white kid had a much smaller black kid forced to his
knees. He was pulling the kid's face to his crotch. The little guy was
fighting back, crying and screaming, but two other big white kids
were restraining him. Then with great force the big kid, hit the little
guy squarely in the face with a clinched fist. Blood from the small
kid's face seemed to splash everywhere. He hit the ground hard.
Several other kids started kicking him and laughing hysterically as he
attempted to escape. One kicked him squarely on the side of the head.

I looked over at Joe and could see tears streaming down his face.
Neither of us had ever seen such brutality and hostility—nothing
even close. I looked back and saw the kid finally break loose and run
in the direction of the railroad tracks some 200 yards away. I looked
for Joe, but he was gone. Then, out of the corner of my eye, I could
see my brother running after the kid. I screamed out Joe's name, and
then ran behind him past soaring bricks. For some reason, no one
was following. Soon we neared the tracks.

Now it was just the kid, my brother Joe, and me. As the kid
approached the tracks, he grabbed a big stone, turned, and screamed
at Joe, "Don't come any closer or I'll throw it." Joe stopped and just
stood there for a moment looking at the kid whose face and shirt were
covered in blood. He wasn't very big, kind of skinny really, but bigger
than Joe. Then Joe did something I'll forever remember.

He started walking slowly toward the kid. Somewhat startled, the kid backed up, falling across the first railroad track and screamed again. "I'll throw it. I mean it. I'll throw it." Joe slowed but continued coming. Then Joe stopped and opened his arms wide. A moment passed, and the rock dropped from the kid's hand. Weeping uncontrollably, he fell into Joe's arms.

They were together in unity draped across the track. Joe held the boy's bleeding head and face against his chest then looked up at me with a look that I will never forget. Soon a peace and calm gently surrounded us. Joe continued to hold him until the boy slowly let go. When finally he left us, he walked down the tracks. Some distance away he turned, stopped, and waved. We waved back.

Years later, Joe and I were returning home in his old run-down Ford from a night in "Old Town" Chicago. Car trouble forced a stop at an obscure South Side gas station. We got out. Six or seven tough looking black guys surrounded us. Then the biggest guy slowly and inquisitively moved to a position face to face with Joe. Though years had passed, their recognition of one another was almost immediate. He smiled as did Joe and then he said to the others. "Fix his car. He's my brother." He and Joe then went and sat on a curb and talked.

As we drove home that early morning, Joe said little.

That early morning no words were necessary.

Most old country neighborhoods had a saw sharpener. My Grandfather (Dziadzia) was that craftsman. As with all artisans, his tools were trustworthy and simple. The real skills needed to do a fine job were, however, in the experienced feel of the hands and arms of the craftsman.

THE SAW SHARPENER

J oe and I, my sister Barbara, and an array of neighborhood kids always liked to watch our grandfather, Dziadzia, work. The wooden saw horse that securely held the saw being worked on was the centerpiece of the crafting endeavor. The many and various files used in his work were kept indoors in the basement. As he considered the work needed to sharpen a saw, he would first take that saw into the basement and then carefully choose the files he wanted and then come back outside to the wooden saw horse.

He seemed to most enjoy his work during the warmest part of summer afternoons. Perhaps in this manner he was less pained by his arthritis. He always donned an old baseball cap, wore a long-sleeved white undershirt, and tied a red bandana around his neck.

He would start out by placing his left foot on an elevated two-by-four of the saw horse. Then with the file placed properly in his hands, he would slowly move the file back and forth. Somewhat, like a golfer following through on his swing, he would lift the file off of the saw as he came to the end of a movement. Eventually, after many such passes, his entire body would flow in a wave-like motion—to and fro, to and fro. Finally, he would turn his attention to each tooth of the saw and then his technique would always be gentler and more relaxed, and the files used would be the smallest and most delicate.

He kept a half-pint of Seagram's in his right back pants pocket, and by the end of a long afternoon two or three saws would have experienced the master's touch and the half-pint would be no more.

The children sitting on the grass in front of him would be mesmerized by the rhythmic, shrill, steel-on-steel symphony of sounds. He would talk to us as he worked and ask us to note the differences in the sounds as the files did their work with each tooth. As he worked, he would explain:

"The hard work that the saw did over time changed it. It has lost its harmony. The work of the files brings that harmony back. Listen to how the sound of the file and the sound of the saw are blending. When that sound becomes one and the scratch is no more, then the tooth of the saw is good. When all of the teeth have the sound of one, the saw is good. It is again in God's harmony. For the carpenter who brought me the saw, work with the saw can once again be a work of joy.

With your own lives, you can sometimes lose the harmony God wanted for you. So find tools that will bring you back. Use them to repair yourself and bring back your harmony and joy."

He would then smile at us, pull his tobacco pouch out from his shirt pocket, roll one, light it, then lean back on his bench and exhale smoke slowly into the summer sky. In that same manner he slowly and intentionally breathed into our lives awareness and love of God's harmony and then patiently and lovingly exhaled it upon us.

All we had to do was to breathe it in.

The story being written is a combination of two true stories. The stories are intertwined. The coach in the story, an Apache leader, is now deceased. He was an exceptional human being and a good friend.

A Captain on God's First Team

Richard had watched his older brother play in division one college football. He thus grew to love the sport. As a young child, Richard's development had been erratic. He did not speak until he was four, then his first words came in full sentences. He could recall and recite full conversations. He could say the alphabet backwards and from memory recite full children's stories backwards, word for word. Yet from age two, loud noises really upset him and he often did not want to be touched. Social interactions and early schooling were tough. Kids seemed to sense his naiveté and vulnerability. He got picked on and humiliated a lot.

During eighth grade he decided to follow his dream. At 5:30 every morning-regardless of inclement weather, he would run along the railroad tracks near his house. Afternoons he would work with weights. He made the football team. He was neither the fastest, nor strongest, but no one tried harder. By his senior year he started on defense and achieved a degree of recognition.

At season's end, he was selected as an alternate to the state all-star football game, which meant that he could play if the selected player could not make it. That happened, so Richard got to go. The game turned out to be a four quarter smash mouth battle. Richard saw little playing time.

At game's end, the coach sought out Richard's parents. "Mr. and Mrs. Simpson, can we talk?" "Certainly, coach." He then said, "Last night our team visited a facility for handicapped children. Once in the facility, our team was introduced to a large group of the handicapped children. For a moment things became extremely awkward and silent. Then, purposefully, one of our players gently nudged his teammates aside, crossed the space between the team and the children, got on the floor, and began playing with these handicapped children. Soon, with delight, the children were all around him—engaged, smiling, touching and hugging him. He then looked up and gestured to his teammates to come forth and join him on the floor. Many did and the awkwardness melted away. As long as I live I will not forget that splendid moment of big football players and the smaller handicapped children on the floor playing together. Needless to say, in that moment there was not an adult dry eye in the facility. It was magic. The player who made this all happen was your son, Richard—a young man who clearly has a sensitivity, and humanity that few possess."

The Simpsons were quite moved. And then the coach went on.

"It's no secret that this will be my last year coaching. I am quite ill. So I pray every day that when I go up there, Ussen (God) will allow me to coach His heavenly team. We all know He has one. And as much as I love these extraordinarily athletic players I have coached, I pray to have a team made up of Richards. After Richard completes his long and productive life and it is finally his time to come, I will look for him. You see, I'll need a defensive captain up there, and I will be holding that spot open for him."

I sit here in my favorite Morgenstern Bloomington bookstore as I take up my pen. The few remaining leaves on the trees, visible out of the bookstore windows, are dancing with the late afternoon sunlight. I write of a love affair that my generation was deeply involved in—a love affair that we had hoped to pass on. In the movie, "The Last Samurai" Tom Cruise is conversing with the young Japanese emperor. The emperor says, "Tell me how he died." Cruise replies, "I will tell you how he lived." So, my friends let me tell you how we lived. Let me share some of the special moments that we experienced as we romanced this country—our America.

"THIS IS MY OWN, MY NATIVE LAND"

I t was 1943 and my grandmother would walk with me to the neighborhood bakery. We would eat a fresh baked donut on the way home. Walking there and back we would pass neighbors sitting on front porches. Conversations would always ensue—most often about the war including questions regarding their enlisted children. Blue star service banners were often prominently centered in the front windows. Occasionally, it was a gold star. I learned early of the difference. By age five I was hesitant to look to the windows of neighbors for fear that yesterday's blue would now be gold, indicating that their son or daughter had given their full measure. Evenings we would lie on the floor near the radio and listen to short wave broadcasts coming out of England. During the days we collected everything for the war effort. Our staples were rationed, but no one seemed to mind. We understood and took pride in the fact that we could contribute.

Then the war ended. Church bells seemed to never end their resounding tintinnabulations; our warriors in uniforms were everywhere and most notable for me, as a child, was observing people spontaneously braking into song everywhere—on buses, on trolleys, in schools, on the way home, in bars, in theaters. If I heard "God Bless America" once in those days I heard it a thousand times. The war was over and we were in love with our country. Little was available so we simply made do. Bailing wire was used on everything.

Interacting with an array of ethnic and racial neighbors was frequent and normal. Few had cars, so walking, old bikes and buses were how you got around.

In 1961 John Kennedy took office. And he said to us all, "Ask not what your country can do for you but rather what can you do for your country." What he said wasn't necessary. For you see, it was the way we felt anyway. During those 60's we attempted to make our contribution to the country we loved. Women's right and civil rights became our focus. Civil rights legislation and Brown v Board of Education became sources of pride. Our parents had secured democracy, and we were attempting to improve its reach to all people.

So what happened? How did we move from "let me contribute" to "What's in it for me?" Are we becoming the "dead souls" spoken of in the passionate poetry of Sir Walter Scott?

"Breathes there the man, with soul so dead, Who never to himself has said, This is my own, my native land."

Our history, though imperfect, is filled with giving, comradeship and love of country. So set aside your animosities, lower your weapons and take up the love affair we had hoped to pass on. Those standing across from you on the artificially created battlefield are your countrymen.

They are us.

The sixteenth hole was a beautiful par three over a pond with tall weeds and cattails around its shores. Golfers completing the fifteenth hole would leave their caddies, take their club of choice and walk the 60 yards to the sixteenth tee. Sixteen was 120 yards long and the green gently slopped toward its back. Many balls fell victim to that slope.

RULES FOR GOLF—RULES FOR LIFE

When I was twelve and my brother Joe was ten, some young
male members of the country club had hired a stripper.
The girl, standing on the sixteenth tee, would expose her breasts or
raise her skirt as golfers would try to drive from that tee. Joe's golfer
decided to have some fun with a young caddy. From the sixteenth tee
he yelled to Joe to bring him another club. I yelled back as I grabbed
the back of Joe's shirt. "I'll bring it." He replied. "I said the little guy."
I yelled back. "He ain't come'in'." The tee, filled with golfers, got silent
as he screamed. "Send him here." I screamed back. "Kiss my a**."
I then grabbed Joe and left the course. The next day, the president
of the Country Club Board called Joe and me to the clubhouse. He
admonished us and told us we should never again swear or curse at
a golfer.

Two weeks later on Tuesday, the women's golf day, I was caddying
for Mrs. Crenshaw. She apparently had asked for me. At the end of
the golf game as we left the eighteen green and were walking toward
the clubhouse she asked, "Are you the young man who objected to
having your little brother go to the vile sixteenth tee?" "Yes ma'am."

"Well, I'm Mrs. Crenshaw, President of the Club's Women's
Auxiliary. The young men who initiated that immoral incident on
sixteen are no longer members of this country club. They clearly didn't
understand our ethical standards and who runs this establishment.
You may share that with your fellow caddies." She then looked down

at me, smiled, and from her flowered change purse handed me an unexpected ten dollar tip.

I loved that eighteenth green, not because of the ten dollar tip, but because in later years as Joe and I were finishing the last round we would ever play on that course, his smile radiated as he lined up his last putt. I believe it was his warm smile that keeps that memory so alive.

We grew up on that country club golf course. I think we grew up in a good way. I believe that the lesson we best learned as we played with poor, but honest fellow caddies and ethical country club members like Mrs. Crenshaw was to never violate the rules.

For a score to be treasured at the end of eighteen holes, you need to know that for all of those holes you never transgressed, you never cheated yourself. And your score in life, like the score on the golf course is laudable only because you worked at following the rules—all of the rules. Rannulph Junuh (Matt Damon) demonstrated this in the movie *Bagger Vance* when he called a stroke on himself because he unintentionally violated a rule by causing his ball to slightly move. He said, "The ball was here and it rolled to here." His young caddy objected, "Only you and me seen it. No one will know." Then Rannulph replied, "I will know Hardy, and so will you."

Maybe life is best lived when simply played like an honest and ethical game of golf.

Just maybe.

Sometime in mid-to-late summer, the Romanian and Ukrainian gypsies came. Their Caravan with horse-drawn wagons would come from the south or the east and onto the large field south of the Standard Steel Car Company—four or five walking minutes from our neighborhood.

CHILDHOOD MEMORIES OF THE VISITING GYPSIES

Their arrival was exciting. Their uniquely designed bowtop wagons with their bright colors of yellow, green, and maroon were for us children much like a moving circus. The caravan's lead wagons were drawn by the very beautiful multi-colored gypsy horses. These docile, athletic, and intelligent horses, though smaller, had the look of the Budweiser draft horses. When the caravan arrived on the field, we would watch in awe as the wagons were circled and the horses unhitched and led off to pasture.

The gypsy wagons were the homes of gypsies and served the commercial function of providing a site for selling and trading. They were usually furnished with a bed, and a small kitchen with some kind of wood burning potbellied stove that vented through the ceiling.

Occasionally, a wagon was constructed in such a way that the exterior wall might be lowered to serve as a way to interrelate with passers-by or customers. Hanging behind the gypsy wagon owner would be such items as painted and decorated pots, specially designed bracelets, golden earrings, and many other additional items for sale or trade. Almost all of what was sold had been made by these gypsies. They were also very skilled at repairing cookware. Aware of such skills, my grandmother and other neighborhood women would routinely bring to the camp broken pots and pans that they could have repaired for a reasonable price.

The "reading wagon," where fortunes were told and tarot cards revealed the future, was ornate and the woodwork was clearly that of a master craftsman. This wagon was a favorite of my grandfather and other carpenters of our neighborhood. They recognized the woodwork as being beyond their skill levels. So, for them it was a joy to observe, and in the manner of a craftsman they would run their hand along the edge of such fine work, then with a smile comment, "jak slicznie" (how beautiful).

Near sundown, when the festivities at the gypsy camp began, a large group of people from the community would arrive to observe the building and lighting of the fire in the center of the circled wagons. They would listen to the music of the mandolins, violins, and accordions, and enjoy the bare-footed dancing of the young gypsy girls in their ornate and colorful skirts and blouses. Within a short time, they would join in the festivities, clapping, cheering, and dancing. My grandfather and our neighbor Mr. Murkowski took no second seat—together, arm over arm in the manner of Zorba the Greek, they would dance.

To Bobby, Stefan, and me the gypsies were most intriguing when, around the night fire, they would share and create folk-lore, folk myths, and gypsy beliefs. We would sit mesmerized, with our eyes wide as the stories were told. We'd never admit it, but walking back to our neighborhood after an evening of listening to those stories was scary. So, we walked with quick looks over our shoulders and got cold chills at any unidentifiable shadowy image.

Sadly, within a week they would be gone.

I so miss the Gypsies. I miss knowing that there existed a people who were that free and full of life. Maybe deep inside of me, they represented a part of my own free soul that I pray I never lose.

I was invited to keynote a criminal justice conference in Miami. Logistical considerations prohibited taking Marion. She suggested, "Why don't you take your dad?" I said, "Do you think he could handle the trip?" "Take a chance. He and you might both enjoy it." I called dad. There was no question about his excitement. He even said that he would bring some golf balls and tees' just in case.

Treasure the Chance Moments with Elderly Parents

We were going to Miami.

Dad had never lost his innocence and love of life. In the plane he wanted a window seat. No six year old's excitement regarding what they were seeing out of the window could hold a candle to his pleasure and enthusiasm. When we got to our room in the hotel we had a very pleasant surprise. Our hotel room had an ocean view—he stared out for the longest time with a never ending smile on his face. We then went to bed early.

At 5:45 am. I was awakened by heavy breathing coming from the direction of dad's bed. Could he be having a heart attack? I looked in his direction. He wasn't in his bed. He was between our beds doing push-ups. "Hey, kid, it's going to be a great day." I was stunned.

Afternoon of the second day we found that the hotel had an agreement with a golf course where guests could play for free. When we arrived at the golf course, we could not be more impressed. It was called the Doral. We entered the pro shop and got in line to secure a tee time—dad with his cut off Bermuda shorts, pipe between his teeth, and a plastic bag in his hand containing our golf balls and tees. I was standing next to him donning my Chicago Cubs baseball cap above the red bandana around my neck. We were strictly class—cover of GQ. It was clear that our presence provoked a deafening hush. Finally, dad said to me in his base-baritone voice, "Hey kid, hell of a lot of clothes in here. Looks like a department store."

When we finally got to the counter to secure a tee time, dad thumped his bag of golf balls and tees on the glass counter. You could cut the tension with a dull knife. "Sir, how can I help you?" Dad replied, "Just need a tee time, young fella, we're from the hotel." The clerk responded with obvious and observable relief. "Sir, your golf course is two miles away. Just go out our main gate and take a left."

We found our course where he suggested. We entered the grounds slowly, for there were quite a few potholes from recent rains, definitely our kind of place. Dad was a fairly good golfer as was I. In years past we had put up some extremely respectable scores. Today however, was just going to be fun. Our drives dribbled off of the tee. We played more frequently in the roughs than the fairways, and we lost a hell of a lot of our golf balls. When down to two, we made a new rule. Find a golf ball on the course, and you could take a stroke off of your score. We laughed a lot that day and enjoyed each other's company. Later in the clubhouse, over some beers, we laughed some more.

Dad is gone now, but when I think back on that chance trip I get kind of choked up and then I smile. So, my friends, if ever you are presented with such an opportunity to be with your parent don't pass it by. It will be a treasure no one can ever take from you. And that special smile on your face will forever belong to you and him or her alone.

Often the beliefs we treasure most are those that we hesitate to talk or write about—rather personal, I suppose. This having been said, I share this very personal experience that I believe (credo) did happen long ago to me. Possibly, a variation of such also happened to you.

A VISION OF HARMONY

On the seminary grounds there was a baseball field high on the hill. If you hit a home run over center field, the ball was pretty much gone forever as the drop-off was significant.

But it was mid-December now and quite cold. I stood alone on the highest point of the hill above the baseball field. The sun was beginning to set and the distant sky was filling with magnificent streaks of oranges, blues, and blacks.

It was the last day of a spiritual retreat. For me it was a good retreat. The formal structure helped with that—the total silence, extended time for reflection, the ancient Gregorian chants, the denial of food, the long periods of being alone. As I remember, I didn't at that moment, have a particular sense of happiness, simply a sense of peace and inner harmony.

Then it happened. I continued to be by myself but felt no longer alone. I felt as though my entire body, soul, and mind were being held—ever so gently. My gaze remained fixated on the setting sun, but then throughout my total cognitive and emotional being I no longer had any questions. I simply understood. There was total and complete cognitive clarity of the entire universe. Everything was so very simple and interrelated. Harmony was in every piece of everything I had ever known and all I had never known. All was part of a whole. It was as if the veil I had unknowingly been wearing all of my life had been momentarily lifted. I could see for the first time, and all was in synchronization and all was good. I had no answers for there were no questions. All was simply understood and part of the whole. Yet there were no parts, simply the understood whole.

And then it was over, as suddenly and unexpectedly as it had began. A millionth part of a moment. For fifty years after this experience, I questioned my worthiness to have received it. Finally, that became clear. What I received was a gift, and somehow, for a reason I shall probably never know, God enjoyed giving it. Did I earn it? As I said, it was a gift. Gifts are gifts. They are not wages paid. They are not owed. I know this clearly now, but still I can't get over wanting to someday give something back—not tit for tat, not I owe you one, not it's my turn, but rather just a gift. The way it was given to me—simply because I'd enjoy doing it.

Did I see the face of God that day? I don't think so. I think he just wanted to show me what he had made and have me, in that instant, understand how everything all fits together.

I believe that someday He'll show it to me again. I hope so. I believe He has shown it to many others, and I know that such of His giving is not infrequent. It's just not something most are comfortable talking about. It seems so very personal. I'm sure that some day He will show it to all of us. I believe it's partially why He created us. He just gets a kick out of sharing things.

In the movie, "Heaven is for Real." A boy about age four clinically dies in the hospital and goes to heaven. Once revived and back home he nonchalantly speaks of things he experienced. "Mom, I didn't know I had a sister."

"Until We Meet Again"

"Of course you do. She's right here." "No, not this sister, the one that died in your tummy. I met her in heaven." "What was her name?" "She didn't have a name; you and dad didn't have time to name her. Oh, there was a beautiful horse in heaven too." "A horse?" "Sure, heaven's full of animals."

For many who saw this movie, it's a sweet fantasy—a fiction. But for me, a hopeless romantic and believer, there's no problem. If I can believe in millions of angels on the head of a pin, then I can certainly believe that miscarried babies and also dogs and cats go to heaven.

Marion and I never owned a cat—dogs a plenty. Then, one late afternoon coming home on a very dark and wooded county road, a shaggy flea bitten scrawny white kitten appeared. We stopped, and Marion opened the door. Without hesitation, he shot into the car. We had a cat. We all said he was lucky so we named him Lucky. We got him to a vet, fed him and cleaned him. He never really ever became totally domesticated, but then neither have I. He seemed a good fit. When we forgot his food or water, he would gently nip Marion in her Achilles heel. Within two years, every one of our married children owned a cat. Funny how that happens.

Patches came along a couple of years later, the runt of a litter from the shelter—a pretend calico. She was sick when we brought her home. For a month she burrowed next to me in my recliner. Once she was well, she would sleep whenever she could, preferably on Marion's lap, or on a bed in the afternoon sun. When wanting to be held, she would follow Marion around the house and utter demanding meows until she was picked up. She was the gentlest of cats and she conversed with you with her eyes. She was always so full of life and pixy sparkle. I personally believe God gives us babies and also these little animals so while on earth we might experience pure honesty, trust, and openness.

One day Lucky went missing. At first we thought he had gotten lost outside, but he had found a remote place in the attic to let life slip away. He was 17 years old. Patches never got over missing him.

Several years later, Patches rather suddenly stopped eating. Marion and I actually attempted to feed her ground up tuna with a toothpick. The medical diagnosis was terrifying—inoperable tumors and the pain would get worse.

When you get to be my age, you have seen death and dying—friends, relatives, and animals. But it is most overwhelming when you are the one deciding when the end will come. She rested in Marion's arms, purring and looking up at us with her gentle eyes. The veterinarian gave her two shots. After the second shot, she continued to look up, but the purring had stopped and gone was the pixy sparkle. We sat quietly holding her for a very long time.

Some day when it is our time, we will head upwards, God willing, and as we gaze out over God's bliss we will meet again. It will be quite easy. For you see, Marion will feel being nipped in her Achilles and simultaneously hear a demanding meow. We will turn, look down, and then peer into their gentle pixy sparkle eyes.

You may believe what you wish, but for us, we are sure God just doesn't let innocent and pure things simply die.

Some things simply cannot be explained for they exist on the edge of real. These three short stories illustrate occurrences near that edge. Each of the stories has as its backdrop Monasteries in the United States and Europe during the later 19th and early 20th centuries.

THE EDGE OF REAL

Joshua

It was 1870 in the upper-Midwest United States. The monastery had been established by European monks. They chose to build on a high hill which afforded them views of the surrounding countryside. They had chosen a fine place for their Order. The grounds surrounding their buildings were perfect for gardening and the planting of fruit trees. A clear river at the base of the largest hill would provide water. Soon the harvests were plentiful but laborers few. So the monks encouraged young men of their faith to enter the monastery with intentions of becoming a brother.

Joshua arrived in twilight. "I would like to be a brother." It was clear that Joshua was lacking both in manner and mind. He was nevertheless accepted provisionally. The following late afternoon at the end of the work day he was given the task of securing two buckets of evening drinking water from the river below. As Joshua climbed the hill with the two full wooden buckets, he tripped and fell. The buckets rolled and bounced down the hill, hitting several large trees and breaking into many pieces. He knelt, wept and prayed at the base of the grotto of the Virgin Mary. The next morning in the monastery he was advised that he would need to leave. With great sadness he did. In the afternoon of that day two young monks were assigned the task of retrieving the broken buckets. They did so and were bringing back the broken pieces. But as they passed the grotto at the top of the hill they found two additional full buckets. This was quite mysterious, since there were only two buckets in the monastery. Joshua was never seen there again.

Mysteriously, monasteries in Brussels and Amsterdam reported of an unassuming and unskilled gentle young man named Joshua seeking work on that very same day. Investigating further, the monks judged that the Joshua encountered in these different location at the same time was the same man.

In the years that followed, the simple, both in manner and mind, were never again turned away from these monasteries.

Jeremiah

Jeremiah was questioning his vocation. He thought that a long evening walk might calm him, so he went out. He walked the older part of the monastery grounds and prayed. At the edge of a red brick path he encountered an old monk.

"Hello, Father. Forgive me, I do not know you."

"I'm Father Sebastian. You appear confused my son."

"I am Father. Can we talk?"

They sat and talked until near dawn. In the morning, more comfortable about his vocation, Jeremiah went to the rector's office.

"Father, I was very confused and fearful of losing my vocation. But I had a long talk with Father Sebastian last night, and everything is now so very clear."

"Jeremiah, we have no Father Sebastian."

"Sure we do Father. That's his picture on the wall behind you."

"Jeremiah, that is a picture of Father Sebastian but he died in 1860 over 70 years ago and is buried in our monastery cemetery at the edge of the red brick path."

Father Caspian

It was early September when a soft banging could be heard in the basement of the four story monastery. Father Caspian, the rector, sent for a plumber. The plumber worked on the furnace and surrounding pipes and the banging stopped. Several weeks later as the monks were at Vespers the banging could again be heard. This time the banging was more intense. The plumber was sent for and came again. He could find nothing wrong. The pounding in the basement continued. A second plumber and his assistant came. After an extensive inspection, they advised the rector that whatever was causing the noise was not coming from the furnace or pipes. Within a week pounding always coming from the basement's west wall and always just before dawn, became deafening. The elderly and wise Friar Dominic had a suggestion—begin saying masses for the dead. Within several days the pounding stopped. The masses continued.

Incidentally, the four-story monastery is not difficult to find. It has a charming garden cemetery for deceased monks that butts up against its west basement wall.

Section Two

Ralph, the Tiniest Leaf

A Very, Very Long Time Ago, there was a little leaf who lived half way up in a big tree. His name was Ralph. He was a nice, happy little leaf. The only thing that made him sad was when some of the bigger leaves on the tree made fun of him because he was so tiny. It really wasn't his fault that he was tiny. He was just born later and hadn't had a chance to grow up yet.

The bigger leaves would often tell stories to each other about the big thunder and rain storms that they lived through when they were little leaves. Ralph wanted to be a part of their memories so bad that he would pretend that he remembered the storms too. But, when he said "Hey, I remember that too," the bigger leaves would say things like, "You weren't even born yet," or, "Be quiet, Ralph," or, worst of all, they sometimes just laughed at him. This made Ralph feel really bad.

Ralph did, however, have one good friend in the tree who never laughed at him—someone who took care of him and watched over him. His name was Old Leaf. Old Leaf lived very high up on the top of the tree and would get really mad at the other bigger leaves when they picked on Ralph. He would tell them to leave Ralph alone, and when he talked they listened to him. There was no leaf on the tree that would disobey or disrespect Old Leaf. Ralph liked Old leaf a lot.

One night when it looked like it was going to become really windy, Old Leaf bent his branch way down and came over to talk to Ralph. Ralph noticed that Old Leaf was no longer green but had turned all different colors and looked really beautiful.

Old Leaf said to Ralph, "Tonight, Ralph, I am going to leave the tree and go down on the ground. But before I go, I wanted to tell you not to be afraid when I am gone and remember that someday you will be a big leaf too and when you are, you will see things that no other leaf on the tree will see because they will all be gone from the tree before you are."

He told Ralph, "Someday, a long time from now it will get very cold and tiny white things will come down from the sky, and after they finish falling from the sky, children will come to play in the white things." Then Old Leaf said, "That's when you should fall from the tree but not before. Remember Ralph, not before. For you see, the children will not come just to play in the white things—they will come to look for you. They will come to look for you because I will have sent them to find you and bring you to me so that we can be together again. Do you believe what I am saying to you, Ralph?' "Yes I do. Yes I do."

"Then believe and have faith. Remember, believe and have faith even when you are tired and begin to doubt. You must have faith and hold on. Do not let go of your branch until you can fall and lie on top of the white things that have fallen."

Ralph didn't really understand what Old Leaf was trying to tell him. Ralph just felt real bad because Old Leaf was leaving the tree. Ralph said, "Please don't go, Old Leaf, please don't go." Ralph felt real bad and he cried that night because he really really liked Old Leaf.

The next morning Ralph looked up to the top of the tree, and he saw that Old leaf was gone. Ralph tried to understand everything that Old Leaf had told him, but he couldn't. All that kept resounding in his mind were the words, "Believe and have faith, Ralph. Believe and have faith."

The days went by and went by, and before Ralph knew it, fall was almost over. Well, you wouldn't believe what happened next. One day Ralph woke up and he looked himself all over and he said, "Hey, I'm a big leaf!" Ralph was so happy he could hardly stand it. He got so excited he shook the whole branch he was on. He almost shook the whole tree. Well, the other leaves said, "Hey, Ralph! Cut it out. You tryin' to knock the tree down?" Ralph looked up at the other leaves and said, "Oh, I'm sorry. I am just really happy because I'm big like you are." And then Ralph noticed that all the other big leaves were all different colors now. They were bright reds, and oranges, shades of browns and greens and magnificent golds and yellows. They really looked beautiful just like Old Leaf did before he left the tree. Ralph didn't understand. He was big like they were, but he was still green like he had always been.

That night there was a terrible storm—one of the worst storms that the tree had ever experienced. The wind blew real hard, and the tree bent a lot. Some of the smaller branches actually cracked and fell to the ground. It stormed and stormed all night. Finally, when it was close to morning, the storm stopped and Ralph opened his eyes. He couldn't believe what he saw. The tree was bare of all its leaves—all but him. He was the only leaf left on the tree. All the other leaves hadn't been able to hold on and had been swept from the tree and fallen to the ground.

Ralph felt very sad. Even though many of them had been mean to him, it was kind of lonely being the only leaf on the tree. At that moment Ralph remembered what Old leaf had told him—he would be the only leaf left on the tree and he would see white things fall down from the sky.

Ralph decided to wait. He waited and waited—day after day, and day after day. But the only thing that happened was that it got colder and colder. It was taking so long that Ralph was beginning to doubt. Ralph was starting to think that the white things would never come. So he said to himself, "Believe and have faith, believe and have faith."

Finally, one cold morning he woke up and stretched and when he looked at his body, he noticed that he had turned colors during the night. He was red and orange and brown and some yellow too. Ralph was really surprised. He said, "Wow! I really look pretty—just like the other big leaves did just before they fell from the tree." Then Ralph thought to himself, "I'll bet I'm going to fall from the tree soon too." He was kind of upset because he hadn't seen the white things from the sky yet.

That night it got really, really cold and windy and Ralph was having a hard time holding onto his branch in the tree. He was just about to let go because he was tired and losing faith. Then it happened. Something fell out of the sky and hit him right on the ear. It kind of went "BLOP." Ralph grabbed it with his hand and looked at it. It was really great. It was completely white and it had beautiful designs all throughout its whiteness—all different designs and "White!" Ralph yelled out. "It's white and it came from the sky." As he looked up and around he could see all kinds of these white things falling from the sky, all white and all with different designs, and all floating past him to the ground—thousands and thousands of them, maybe millions. Ralph was so excited that he just hung onto the tree all night. It was hard to hold on because it was so cold and he was really tired. But Old Leaf had told him to hold on, so he did as he watched the pretty white things fall and swirl to the ground.

In the morning the white things had stopped falling and the whole ground was white and everything looked so beautiful. Far away in the distance Ralph could see four children walking toward his tree and playing in the white stuff that fell from the sky. They sure were having fun throwing it around and kicking it with their boots. When they got close to the tree, Ralph could see that two of the children were little girls and two were little boys. But at this moment, Ralph was getting awfully tired of holding onto the tree. He was exhausted. So he decided that this must be the time Old Leaf wanted him to let go. So he did. Ralph felt himself floating.

Floating, and floating, and floating all the way down. Floating and floating right down to the white stuff on the ground. Ralph landed right in front of one of the children. "Look," she said. "Look at the beautiful leaf that didn't get covered by the snow!" Another child said, "It must be the really special one that Old Leaf told us to look for and bring home. Let's pick it up very gently and take it home and put it in our special place." They bent over and picked up Ralph and held him gently in their hands.

That evening the children all gathered happily in the living room around Ralph. They said, "Now pick him up gently and take him to the Christmas tree and put him next to Old Leaf." "Yes, that's it. That's it. Look how beautiful they look together."

Ralph looked up into the eyes of old leaf and Old Leaf smiled. Ralph could not be happier. He continued to look up at Old Leaf next to him and Old Leaf continued to smile and look down at him. Then Old Leaf put his long arm around Ralph and Ralph felt warm all over—the kind of warm that wraps around you on a perfect winter afternoon when crisp is in the air and the smells of God's beautiful winter world fills your whole inside. Now Ralph understood. None of the bad things that ever happened to him mattered. They didn't matter at all. All that mattered was the laughter and joy of the children, Old Leaf, and that very warm feeling that he felt inside and all over.

The words he had been taught by Old Leaf so long ago resonated through his whole body and little soul,

"Believe and have faith Ralph, believe and have faith."

SECTION THREE

ABOUT THE AUTHORS

R aymond J Golarz holds a BA degree in Sociology and a BS degree in Education from St. Joseph's College in Indiana. He received his master's degree and his doctorate degree in Education from Indiana University. He taught middle school and high school and then served as the Director of Child Welfare Services where he supervised delinquency prevention and intervention programs and worked with the very poor and with delinquent gangs in the same neighborhoods where he spent his early childhood.

He taught psychology at St. Joseph's College, Purdue Calumet, Indiana University Northwest, and City College in Seattle. In addition, near Chicago he also taught Psychology for Law Enforcement for nearly ten years. He has been an assistant superintendent and superintendent of public schools. He enjoys keynoting and has keynoted for school districts and major conferences in virtually every state in the United States and in most of the Canadian Provinces.

He is a co-author of *Restructuring Schools for Excellence through Teacher Empowerment. He is the* author of *Yellow Jacket Football In Hard Times and Good* and a companion book *When the Yellow Jackets Played.* These two books, using the backdrop of rugged American sandlot semi-pro football near Chicago, focus on the strengths of the early immigrants who came to America and, with their children, lived through the challenges of the Great Depression. With his wife Marion he Co-authored *On My Way Home I Bumped Into God, Sweet Land of Liberty, The Power of Participation, The Problem Isn't Teachers,* and *A Teacher's Storybook.*

All of his life, Ray has enjoyed sketching, oil painting, and woodworking. He and his wife Marion reside in Bloomington, Indiana.

Marion Simpson Golarz, the sixth of seven children, was born to Michael and Marion Simpson in 1940 in the quiet, Lake Erie town of Conneaut, Ohio.

Marion secured a BA in English Language Arts, and an MS in Education with a concentration in Reading from Indiana University. She taught English and remedial reading at the elementary and secondary levels as well as composition courses at Indiana University Northwest, Indiana University Southeast, and Purdue University Calumet where she also taught in the Writing Lab.

With her husband Raymond she has co-authored five books. *On My Way Home I Bumped into God, The Problem Isn't Teachers, Sweet land of Liberty, The Power of Participation.* and *A Teacher's Storybook.* They recently celebrated 50 years of marriage with their six children and their families, including 10 grandchildren.

Almost all of her personal writings began with thoughts written on the backs of napkins and scraps of paper. She has forever written poetry and prose. She reads virtually anything she can get her hands on with her Boxer pup Cooper lying at her feet.

The email address for Ray and Marion is mjgolarz@live.com.

Printed in the United States
by Baker & Taylor Publisher Services